MORRIS L. VENDEN

Y0-CDM-127

95 THESES*
on Righteousness by Faith

*Apologies to Martin Luther

Pacific Press Publishing Association
Boise, Idaho
Oshawa, Ontario, Canada

Edited by B. Russell Holt
Designed by Tim Larson
Cover illustration by Consuelo Udave
Type set in 10/12 Century Schoolbook

ISBN 0-8163-1081-5

91 92 ● 6 5 4 3

Contents

Introduction

Actually, there is little need to apologize to Martin Luther! His flash of insight on the famous staircase, that the just shall live by faith, was indeed a major landmark in the Protestant Reformation. But the 95 theses that he nailed to the door of the church in Wittenberg were not primarily a further discussion of the subject of justification by faith. Instead, they dealt primarily with necessary reforms in the religious system of the day, insisting on freedom of conscience, condemning the sale of indulgences, and thundering against papal abuses.

The 95 theses in this volume are centered on the truths of righteousness by faith in Jesus Christ alone. It is a message of timeless application, ever on the crescendo, until the time when one interest prevails, one subject swallows up all other subjects, Christ our righteousness. We live in that day. The message of the three angels has been sounded and will continue to resound until it reaches loud cry proportions.

The purpose of this book is to encourage thought and study on the great theme of the righteousness of Christ. It is written primarily for a Seventh-day Adventist audience, with a companion set of Bible lessons designed for sharing with your friends.

But be careful! If you find yourself agreeing with even the first thesis, you may be hooked. If you still find yourself in agreement after the first twelve theses, there's no escape! Anyone who really agrees with the first twelve theses is going to be hard-pressed to disagree with the rest, for the first twelve form the basis of understanding for the whole package.

The theory of righteousness by faith is dynamite. Once you really understand it, you are never the same. But the theory is not enough. The real power comes as you *experience* it for yourself. I invite you today to the experience of a lifetime!

95 Theses on Righteousness by Faith

Righteousness

1. A Christian does what is right *because* he is a Christian, never *in order* to be one. John 15:5.
2. Righteousness equals Jesus. We have no righteousness apart from Him. Romans 1:16, 17.
3. The only way to seek righteousness is to seek Jesus. Romans 4:4, 5.
4. Christianity and salvation are not based on what you *do* but on whom you *know*. Romans 3:28.
5. Doing right by not doing wrong is not doing right. Being good by not being bad is not being good. Matthew 23:27, 28.
6. Righteousness will make you moral, but morality will not make you righteous. Matthew 5:20.
7. Our good works have nothing to do with *causing* us to be saved. Our bad works have nothing to do with *causing* us to be lost. Romans 3:20.

Sin

8. Everyone is born sinful (or self-centered) because everyone is born separated from God. Psalm 58:3.
9. God does not hold us accountable for being born sinful. Ezekiel 18:20; John 1:9.
10. We sin because we are sinful. We are not sinful because

we sin. Romans 7:14-17.

11. Sin (singular)—living apart from God, results in sins (plural)—doing wrong things. 1 John 3:4.

12. Whoever lives life apart from God is living in sin. John 16:8, 9.

Faith

13. The best definition for faith is trust. Faith is depending upon another. Matthew 15:21-28.

14. Knowing God results in trusting God. If you don't know Him, you won't trust Him. If you don't trust Him, you don't know Him. 2 Timothy 1:12.

15. Faith is a fruit of the Spirit, not a fruit of the person. It is not something we work on, or work up. Galatians 5:22.

16. Positive thinking does not produce genuine faith, but faith will produce positive thinking. Romans 10:17.

Surrender

17. Surrender is giving up on ourselves, not giving up our sins. Giving up our sins is the result of giving up on ourselves and seeking God. Romans 10:3, 4.

18. Working to give up our sins can keep us from giving up on ourselves. Romans 9:31, 32.

19. No one can crucify or bring himself to surrender. Someone else must do that for him. Galatians 2:20.

20. We are controlled by God or Satan. The only control we have is to choose who will control us. Romans 6:16.

21. The surrender of the will is the surrender of the power of choice, but we use our power of choice to surrender it. We give up our power of choice toward behavior; we keep our power of choice toward relationship. Philippians 2:13; Romans 6:11.

22. The only *deliberate* effort in the Christian life is to seek God. Spontaneous effort toward other things will result. John 15:5; Philippians 4:13.

23. Growing Christians experience on-again, off-again sur-

render. Sometimes they depend on God, sometimes on themselves. Luke 9:54; Matthew 16:16, 17, 22, 23.

Conversion

24. Conversion is the work of the Holy Spirit, which produces a change of attitude toward God and creates a new capacity for knowing God. John 3:3-8.
25. Conversion leads to a changed life. Ezekiel 36:26, 27.
26. Conversion and repentance are continuing experiences, not once only. Luke 9:23.

Repentance

27. Repentance is sorrow for sin and turning away from sins. Repentance is a gift. Therefore, sorrow for sin is a gift, and turning away from sins is a gift. Acts 5:31.
28. We do not change our lives in order to come to Christ. We come to Him just as we are, and He changes our lives. John 6:37.
29. God gives us repentance *before* He gives forgiveness. Acts 3:19.
30. Worldly sorrow is being sorry we broke a law and got caught. Godly sorrow is being sorry we broke a heart and hurt our best Friend. 2 Corinthians 7:10.

Forgiveness

31. The only known sin that can't be forgiven is the one for which we don't repent and ask forgiveness. 1 John 1:9.
32. Forgiveness does the sinner no good unless he accepts it. Psalm 86:5.
33. God's forgiveness is not limited, but our acceptance of His forgiveness can be. Matthew 18:21, 22.
34. Those who are forgiven much will love much. Those who love much will obey much. Luke 7:41-43; John 14:15.
35. Forgiveness is free, but it is not cheap. It cost the life of God's dear Son. John 3:16.

The Cross

36. God forgives sinners, not sins, but the Bible calls this the forgiveness of sins. Jesus died because sins could not be forgiven. Isaiah 53:5, 6, 8.
37. Christ died for our sins according to the Scripture. 1 Corinthians 15:3.
38. The cross made it possible for God to be just and yet to forgive anyone. Romans 3:23-26.
39. The death of Christ was necessary in order for us to be forgiven. John 3:14, 15.
40. We can add nothing to what Jesus did at the cross, but God can add plenty. Hebrews 7:25; 9:11, 12.

Assurance

41. Staying with Jesus is just as important as coming to Him. John 15:4.
42. Assurance of salvation continues through the daily personal relationship with Jesus. 1 John 5:11, 12.
43. Christians should know that they have the assurance of salvation today. John 6:47.
44. The Bible teaches once-saved always-saved as long as you keep saved. Matthew 24:12, 13.
45. Peace does not come from victory, but victory comes from peace. John 8:11.
46. One reason we keep sinning is that we don't believe we are forgiven. Assurance leads to victory. Uncertainty leads to defeat. 1 John 3:2, 3.

Relationship

47. Righteousness by faith is an experience, not just a theory. Philippians 3:9, 10.
48. The Christian's devotional life is not optional. The relationship with God is the entire basis of the ongoing Christian life. John 17:3.
49. If we don't regularly take time for the Bible and prayer

we will eventually die spiritually. John 6:53.

50. Just because you read the Bible and pray doesn't mean you'll have a relationship with God, but if you don't, you won't. John 5:39.

51. The primary purpose of prayer is not to get answers but to know Jesus. Revelation 3:20; John 17:3.

52. The primary purpose of Bible study is not to get information but to know Jesus. Revelation 3:20.

53. Things often go worse when we pray until we learn to seek Jesus for His sake, not ours. Job.

54. Anyone who gets discouraged with his relationship because of his behavior is a legalist. Romans 7:14-24.

Obedience

55. True obedience is a gift from God (the robe is free!). Matthew 22:11-14.

56. Real obedience comes from the inside out, not from the outside in. Matthew 23:25, 26.

57. Genuine obedience is natural and spontaneous. It comes only through the faith relationship with Christ. John 14:15.

58. One who is depending on God for power doesn't have to try hard to obey. He would have to try hard not to obey. 1 John 3:6.

59. Obedience that is only external is false obedience. Matthew 5:20.

60. When we know God as it is our privilege to know Him, our lives will be lives of continual obedience. 1 John 2:3.

Law

61. Anyone who tries to live the Christian life apart from Christ is not a Christian. He is a legalist, whether conservative or liberal. Galatians 3:1-3.

62. There is no power for genuine obedience in the law. Mount Sinai is no good without Mount Calvary. Romans 8:3.

63. Christ is the end of the law for righteousness, but not the end of the law. Romans 10:4.

Works

64. Good works done apart from Christ are bad works. Matthew 7:22, 23.
65. The purpose of good works is not to save us, but to bring glory to God. Matthew 5:16.
66. When it comes to genuine faith and works, you can't have one without the other. James 2:17, 18, 26.

Growth

67. Faith grows in quantity, not quality. Growth is in the constancy of dependence upon God. Luke 17:5, 6.
68. You don't grow by trying to grow. Matthew 6:27.
69. Christians grow stronger by realizing their weakness. When they are weak, then they are strong. 2 Corinthians 12:9, 10.
70. We can do all things through Christ who strengthens us, but without Him we can do nothing. Philippians 4:13; John 15:5.

Abiding

71. Satan has no power to cause those who depend on God to sin, but those who depend on themselves are easily defeated. 2 Corinthians 10:4, 5.
72. The abiding daily relationship with God leads to an abiding surrender, moment-by-moment dependence on Him. John 15:1-5.
73. Looking to self is always the point of separation from God and breaks the moment-by-moment dependence on Him. Matthew 14:28-30.
74. God will never separate from us, but we can choose to separate from God. Romans 8:35, 38, 39.

Witness

75. The reason God wants us to witness is primarily for our good. Matthew 11:29.
76. The desire to share comes naturally for the genuine Christian (although methods may vary). 2 Corinthians 4:13.
77. The happiest person in the world is the one most involved in serving others. The most miserable person is the one most involved in serving self. Mark 8:35.
78. Christian service in the spiritual life corresponds to exercise in the physical life. Acts 3:6-9.
79. We cannot give to others that which we do not ourselves possess. Mark 5:19; John 3:11.

Temptation

80. The real issue in temptation is whether to live life apart from Christ. John 16:8, 9.
81. Temptations become sins when we consent to them in our minds. Matthew 5:21, 22, 28.
82. Jesus was tempted to do right, but in His own power, and so are we. Matthew 4:2, 3.
83. The Lord knows how to deliver the godly out of temptations, but not the ungodly. 2 Peter 2:9.
84. Temptations are not overcome at the time of temptation, but always before. Hebrews 4:16.

Victory

85. Victory is not something we achieve. It is something we receive. 1 Corinthians 15:57.
86. In the Christian warfare we are active toward the fight of faith and passive toward the fight of sins. Ephesians 6:10-18.
87. Real victory is getting the victory over trying to get the victory. 2 Chronicles 20:15, 17.

Perfection

88. Perfection of character is not our work. It is God's work
in us. Hebrews 13:20, 21.
89. Perfection can be a dangerous topic if it focuses our attention on ourselves and our own works. Galatians 3:3.

Jesus

90. Jesus was like Adam before the fall in that He had a sinless nature—He was not born separated from God. Jesus
was like Adam after the fall in physical strength, mental
power, and moral worth (backbone). Luke 1:35; Hebrews
2:17, 18.
91. Jesus had no advantage over us in overcoming temptations. Hebrews 4:15.
92. Jesus overcame temptations the same way we can overcome: by power from above rather than power from
within. John 14:10.
93. Jesus found sins repulsive. So long as we depend on God,
we also find sins repulsive. Hebrews 1:8, 9.
94. We can never *be* as Jesus was, but we can *do* as Jesus did.
John 14:12.
95. The problem of sin is a broken relationship between God
and man. The goal of salvation is to restore the relationship between God and man. Revelation 19:7-9.

Thesis 1

A Christian does what is right because he is a Christian, never in order to be one.

It happened during the first few weeks in a new parish. At this church, my goal was to visit every family to begin getting acquainted. But it's easy to stop with just small talk. "Is that Aunt Minnie's picture up there on the mantle?"

"Yes."

So I came up with a gimmick: one question, the same question, asked at each home. "What is your definition of a Christian?" And I kept a careful record of each response.

"A Christian is one who lives by the golden rule."

"A Christian is honest."

"A Christian is someone who is kind and loving."

"A Christian is a good neighbor."

I heard many different answers, but one common denominator. Every answer was a behavioral answer. The name of Christ was conspicuously absent.

You can read reports of newsmen interviewing the man on the street, asking similar questions. The pattern of answers is the same.

"A Christian does this, and does that. A Christian doesn't do the other thing." How often do you hear the response, "A Christian is one who knows and loves Christ?"

What *is* Christianity? Is it primarily based on behavior? Or is it primarily based on relationship? Here is the bottom line for understanding and experiencing salvation by faith in Christ. Christianity is a matter of knowing Christ. And the behavior which distinguishes the Christian from the non-Christian

15

comes as a *result* of the faith relationship with Jesus—it is never the cause.

Let's rephrase this thesis just a bit. An apple tree bears apples because it is an apple tree, never in order to be one. Jesus made the same comparison: "Every good tree bringeth forth good fruit; but a corrupt tree bringeth forth evil fruit. A good tree cannot bring forth evil fruit, neither can a corrupt tree bring forth good fruit." Matthew 7:17, 18.

If you're interested in good fruit, the starting place is a good tree. Your task, then, is to water the tree, fertilize it perhaps, and allow the sun and rain and wind to do their work. There is no need to try hard to produce fruit. If you have a healthy tree, the fruit will come as a matter of course.

That's how it is in the Christian life. The one who tries to live the Christian life by working on behavior is on a dead-end street. *Christ's Object Lessons* puts it this way: "It is by the renewing of the heart that the grace of God works to transform the life. No mere external change is sufficient to bring us into harmony with God. There are many who try to reform by correcting this or that bad habit, and they hope in this way to become Christians, but they are beginning in the wrong place. Our first work is with the heart."—Page 97.

No matter how upright your life may be, no matter how many good deeds you may perform, no matter how religious you may appear, you are not a genuine Christian until you know Jesus Christ personally, one-to-one. Doing what is right will never make you a Christian. It will only make you moral.

The early church focused so on the Lord Jesus Christ that He was the theme of their thought and conversation. "Christ did this, and Christ said that." Finally someone said, "Let's just call them *Christ*–ians."

What would you be called if you were named according to the thing you speak and think of the most? Are you a good person? Or are you really a Christian? Think about it!

Thesis 2

Righteousness = Jesus. We have no righteousness apart from Him.

My major professor in college opened the class discussion during the first class period of the semester by asking us for a definition of *righteousness.*

We offered many definitions. Righteousness is right doing. Righteousness is conformity to the law of God. Righteousness is holiness. And perhaps even better, righteousness is love. Not only did class members give these definitions, but you can find such definitions in the inspired commentary.

But after the professor had frustrated us into thinking of every possible definition, he finally brought us to the conclusion that the best, most complete definition for righteousness is Jesus. All other definitions are inadequate.

If, for instance, righteousness is defined as right doing, then the only thing you would need to be righteous would be—what? To do what is right. You would have no need for a Saviour if righteousness were based on behavior alone.

But righteousness is not an entity in itself. It is not something that mankind can produce in any way. We are bankrupt of righteousness. Isaiah says, "All our righteousnesses are as filthy rags." Isaiah 64:6. Not only are we unable to produce righteousness, but we are also incapable of stockpiling it. It isn't something we can obtain or retain apart from Jesus. Therefore, we can best define righteousness as a Person. So long as we have Jesus, we have righteousness. But without Him, we have no hope for righteousness.

"Sinful man can find hope and righteousness only in God,

17

and no human being is righteous any longer than he has faith in God and maintains a vital connection with Him."—*Testimonies to Ministers,* p. 367.

You might try it in the form of an equation. If Jesus = Righteousness, and Righteousness = Jesus, then the only way we can obtain righteousness is to get with Jesus, and stay with Him. So we might say that Mankind + Jesus = Righteousness.

I was discussing this with a group of college students one day when a young man in the back row got this strange look on his face. He raised his hand and said, "But if Jesus equals righteousness all by Himself, and if mankind plus Jesus equals righteousness, then mankind equals nothing!" And he spoke as if I had just done a great injustice to the human race.

But isn't it the dilemma of mankind that we have no righteousness of our own? We are worth everything in the eyes of heaven. Jesus on the cross proved the worth of the human soul. But when it comes to producing righteousness, we are helpless. We cannot produce it; we have none.

Charles T. Everson told the story of a woman who went shopping for material to make a new dress. She fingered the fabric, examined the weave, admired the colors and patterns, until she finally found one bolt of cloth that seemed to be what she wanted. As she still hesitated, wanting to make sure of her choice, the proprieter of the store approached and said, "I've noticed you looking at that material, and it just so happens that that particular piece has been made up into a dress. Perhaps you didn't notice it as you came in."

So they went together to the display window in the front of the store, and the woman exclaimed, "It's beautiful! It's exactly what I want. It was lovely material—but now that I see it made up into a dress, I'm completely convinced." And she purchased the material.

That's how it is with God's law. We can admire its principles; we can agree with its precepts. But before we can truly appreciate and accept it, we must see it made up into a life—the life of Jesus. When we see Him, our hearts are won. And when we receive Him, we receive His righteousness as well.

Thesis 3

The only way to seek righteousness is to seek Jesus.

Once upon a time there was a man who wanted to become a baker. He had always loved fresh-baked bread, and he thought he would enjoy baking it for others.

So he checked around town for the best location for a new business. He got a corner lot, hired the town contractor, and soon had his bakery ready to open, with gleaming stainless steel sinks and appliances in back, and shining glass cases in front to display his wares.

But things didn't go too well for the baker. He worked long hours. He advertised every way he could think of. He tried his best to make a go of it. Yet he couldn't seem to produce the kind of bread he had tasted in the past. When customers came by to see his new building, they seldom purchased any of his wares. And they never returned.

Finally, after years of struggling, he had to admit he was a failure. He was at the point of bankruptcy. He had tried everything he knew to make his bakery successful, and nothing had worked.

Just when he was ready to give it up completely, he heard about something that revolutionized his entire business. He learned that in order to make bread he needed *flour!* He hadn't tried that before, but somehow it sounded good to him. And when he began using flour, it made all the difference.

Have you guessed that this is a parable? We would find it hard to believe that anyone could really overlook the simple, basic truth that it takes flour to make bread. We realize it would be tragic to try to run a bakery without it.

No matter what business you are in, you have to understand certain basic requirements if you ever hope to succeed. You can't keep a bank going without money. You can't run a railroad with only cabooses. It's impossible to raise wool if you have no sheep.

But what about living the Christian life? How many of us have overlooked the basics for years? Seeking for righteousness, but not knowing how to obtain it? And it is nothing but frustrating to try to be a Christian without understanding how to accomplish it.

The newsmen have certain leading questions they ask in order to get down to the basics of a news story. These questions can be transferred to the Christian life. The first is What? Sometimes it's easiest to talk about the *what* of the Christian life. Some of us grew up on *what*. What to do, and what not to do in order to be a Christian and in order to be saved. We had a pretty heavy diet of that. It led to discussions in academy Bible classes and weeks of prayer, asking what's wrong with this, and what's wrong with that?

Is it wrong to talk about *what?* No, the Bible contains much information about *what*. But *what* can never be the basis of Christianity.

Then there's the question of Why? That's the sophisticated, intellectual question. That's where you analyze and dissect and discuss. That's the best question to fill up time in the Sabbath School lesson study period. *Why* can be important. God says, "Come now, and let us reason together." Isaiah 1:18. It's not wrong to reason. We are born in God's image, with the ability to think and consider. But *why* is not enough.

Another question we have spent a lot of time with in the history of our church is the question of When? When is it all going to happen? And so we have the charts on the wall telling about *when*. Perhaps some are so interested in the *when* because they are hoping to get on the last trolley out. But others worry that the *when* will catch up with them before they figure out *how* to do the *what?*

If you grew up on *what* and *why* and *when,* the next logical question is How? It's a practical question, and it can lead you into the theory of righteousness by faith. If you don't understand *how*, the rest will only frustrate you. But even knowing *how* is not enough, because righteousness by faith is more than a theory. It is an experience. And *how* becomes a most exciting question when you understand that the answer to *how* is *who!*

Jesus is the basis of Christianity. It is true the Bible talks about seeking righteousness. Zephaniah 2:3 says it in so many words, "Seek righteousness." And some of us have thought that the way to seek Jesus is to seek righteousness. But we missed the *how*. Since Righteousness = Jesus, the way to seek righteousness is to seek Jesus. "The righteousness of God is embodied in Christ. We receive righteousness by receiving Him."—*Mount of Blessing,* p. 18.

Thesis 4

Christianity and Salvation are not based on what you do but on whom you know.

A woman bought a new pair of contact lenses. Not long after, she was stopped for a traffic violation, and the police officer, after looking at the restriction on her driver's license asked sternly, "Where are your glasses?"

She replied, "I have contacts."

He said, "I don't care whom you know—you're supposed to be wearing your glasses!"

It's an indisputable fact in this world that whom you know makes a difference. If you're looking for employment and you're acquainted with the boss, you have an advantage. If you're brought into court and you know the judge, it's good news. If you're wishing for an introduction to someone, and you discover that you know his friend, you've got it made.

When Abraham Lincoln was president, he would sometimes leave instructions with his staff that he was not to be disturbed. He would go into his office and close the door behind him. The guards would stand outside, and up and down the hallway, to prevent anyone from going in.

But then someone would come hurrying down the hall. He would walk right past the guards, throw open the door, and go straight to the president. The guards wouldn't even try to stop him. Why? Because his name was Tad Lincoln, and he was the president's son! His relationship to the president made all the difference.

Do you believe that your relationship with Christ is the thing that makes all the difference in your spiritual life? Do you believe that Christianity is based on whom you know? Or do you believe that it is based on what you do?

At a camp meeting in the Northwest several years ago, the editor of the *Adventist Review* stood up and asked the audience some questions. He said, "How many of you believe that you are saved by faith in Jesus Christ alone?" A few hands went up and then quickly back down.

Then he asked, "How many of you believe that you are saved on the basis of your works?" A few other hands went up and then quickly back down.

And he asked, "How many of you believe that you are saved by faith in Jesus Christ, plus your good works?" And all the rest of the hands went up and stayed up and waved in the air!

He said, "I hope by the time this morning's sermon is over, you will have changed your minds!" And he went on to prove that we are saved by faith in Christ alone. Period.

Jesus said it in John 17:3: "This is life eternal, that they might know thee the only true God, and Jesus Christ, whom thou hast sent." *The Desire of Ages,* page 331 says, "As through Jesus we enter into rest, heaven begins here. We respond to His invitation, Come, learn of Me, and in thus coming we begin the life eternal. Heaven is a ceaseless approaching to God through Christ."

Do you know Him? Knowing Jesus is the entire basis of the Christian life. Knowing Jesus is the way to life eternal. Knowing Jesus will change your lifestyle, for as you learn to know Him and love Him and associate with Him, you will be changed into His image.

Righteousness is a Person. Salvation is a Person. Through Jesus your eternal life can start today!

Thesis 5

Doing right by not doing wrong is not doing right. Being good by not being bad is not being good.

If you're not doing anything wrong, then you're doing right, right? Wrong!

Of course, this does not mean that if you're doing wrong you're doing right, or that it's all right to do wrong. What it does mean is that you can be doing right on the outside, but wrong on the inside. And that's not right! The only one who really does what's right is the one who is right on the inside as well as on the outside.

Have you ever heard of the Pharisees? Were they right or wrong? Jesus spoke some strong words to the Pharisees in Matthew 23:27, 28. "Woe unto you, scribes and Pharisees, hypocrites! for ye are like unto whited sepulchres, which indeed appear beautiful outward, but are within full of dead men's bones, and of all uncleanness. Even so ye also outwardly appear righteous unto men, but within ye are full of hypocrisy and iniquity."

Which brings us to an important question. While we can agree that the goal for the Christian is to be good both on the inside *and* on the outside, suppose you're not good on the inside yet? Aren't you better off at least being good on the outside, if that's the best you can do? Isn't being a Pharisee better than being a publican? Be careful how you answer!

Jesus said that the religion of the Pharisee was not sufficient for eternal life. "Except your righteousness shall exceed the righteousness of the scribes and Pharisees, ye shall in no case enter into the kingdom of heaven." Matthew 5:20. So whatever external goodness is good for, it's no good for salvation.

We might look at *Steps to Christ,* page 44. "There are those who profess to serve God, while they rely upon their own efforts to obey His law, to form a right character, and secure salvation. Their hearts are not moved by any deep sense of the love of Christ, but they seek to perform the duties of the Christian life as that which God requires of them in order to gain heaven. Such religion is worth nothing." So whatever external goodness is good for, it's no good for religion. It's worth nothing there.

In Revelation 3 is a special message to the church for the time just before Jesus comes again. "I know thy works, that thou art neither cold nor hot: I would thou wert cold or hot. So then because thou art lukewarm, and neither cold nor hot, I will spue thee out of my mouth." Verses 15, 16. So whatever external goodness is good for, it's worse in God's estimation than no goodness at all! He prefers even cold to lukewarm!

Goodness that is only external is repulsive to God. He knows that the open sinner is more easily reached with the good news of salvation than the one who feels no need. Those who succeed in being good on the outside in their own strength are isolated from needing a Saviour. And since they feel no need, they don't come to Christ to receive the salvation He's waiting to give.

It is possible to fill the church with strong people who are able to produce the behavior that the church requires. And the behavior of which they are so proud becomes a barrier against any personal relationship with Jesus Christ.

If we really believed this, if we really accepted the thesis that outward righteousness is not only worthless in the eyes of God, but actually distasteful to Him, we would stop *trying* to do what is right! Instead, we would put our time and energy and effort toward seeking Him, that He might come and live His life in us.

Does it scare you? Are you afraid to give up trying to do what's right? Are you willing to put your effort toward accepting His righteousness day by day in an ongoing relationship with Him? If you're feeling nervous here, wondering where behavior comes in, hurry up and read the next chapter. It begins, "Righteousness will make you moral." Quickly now, go to the next page!

Thesis 6

Righteousness will make you moral, but morality will not make you righteous.

God is not against morality! He doesn't rebuke the Laodiceans in Revelation 3 because of their morality. He rebukes them because they are trying to substitute morality for righteousness.

You may not be against plastic grapes! You may find them very attractive when arranged in a centerpiece. There is a place for plastic fruit, and some of the imitations on the market are quite convincing. But when someone adds plastic grapes to the fruit salad, you are sure to find them disappointing and distasteful. They are no substitute for real fruit.

God is not against morality! If you are living a moral life, you will stay out of jail. You won't make oatmeal out of your brain. You will hold a job better. Your reputation and standing in the community will improve. Those around you won't suffer the effects of your immoral behavior. Morality has some real advantages, no question about it. But God's rebuke to the Laodicean church is based on the premise that morality is never a substitute for righteousness.

"Many who call themselves Christians are mere human moralists."—*Christ's Object Lessons,* p. 315. Notice that this is not describing those who call themselves human moralists. It's describing ones who call themselves Christians, but who are not.

In the parable of the man without a wedding garment (See Matthew 22), we see the same principle. The man could have chosen to stay home from the wedding where his citizen's dress would have excited no comment. The king invited him to the wedding, but didn't force him to attend. The man's problem was that he tried to substitute his own clothes for the robe the king provided and still make it in to the wedding.

The people in the days of Christ had perfected a religion based on morality alone. The Pharisee who prayed standing in the temple was a victim of morality as a substitute for righteousness. He was beating his own moral drum. He recited to God a list of the deeds that he felt would recommend him to heaven. He based his security on the fact that he didn't *do* what the publican *did*. He was a behaviorist.

And he proved again that not only will morality fail to make you righteous, it can actually keep you from genuine righteousness.

God is not against morality! Read it in *Steps to Christ,* page 18. "Education, culture, the exercise of the will, human effort, all have their proper sphere, but here they are powerless. They may produce an outward correctness of behavior, but they cannot change the heart."

We shouldn't discard morality, but we need to properly understand it. Morality is a result of righteousness. It is not a cause of righteousness. It is never a cause. The genuine Christian will be a moral person. In seeking genuine righteousness, we need never fear that morality will be left out. It is possible to have external goodness all by itelf, but it is never possible to have internal goodness alone. When the heart is changed, the inevitable result will be a change of behavior. Righteousness will always make you moral. "If we abide in Christ, if the love of God dwells in us, our feelings, our thoughts, our purposes, our actions, will be in harmony with the will of God as expressed in the precepts of His holy law."—*Steps to Christ,* p. 61.

God is not against morality! But he warns us against accepting morality as a substitute for righteousness. He invites us to accept, instead, the righteousness of Christ, freely given to all who come unto God by Him.

Thesis 7

Our good works have nothing to do with *causing* us to be saved. Our bad works have nothing to do with *causing* us to be lost.

Elder A. T. Jones was one of the champions of righteousness by faith in Christ alone during the 1888 emphasis within our church. He was evidently a fiery speaker and quite an individualist. In his enthusiasm he had overstated his case, and the Lord sent him a message of counsel. It's found in *Selected Messages,* book 1, beginning on page 377.

Elder Jones had several times stated that good works amount to nothing, that there are no conditions to salvation. Ellen White told him, "I know your meaning, but you leave a wrong impression upon many minds. While good works will not save even one soul, yet it is impossible for even one soul to be saved without good works."—Page 377. And just a few pages later in the same volume, page 388, she says, "Works will not buy for us an entrance into heaven."

So where did Elder Jones overstate his case? What is the difference between saying that good works amount to nothing and saying that good works will not save even one soul, nor buy an entrance into heaven?

Some people jump to the conclusion that if good works do not save us, then they must not be important. And if our bad works don't cause us to be lost, then bad deeds must be OK. But one key word prevents this kind of misunderstanding. In talking about the relationship of our good or bad deeds in causing us to be saved or lost, don't miss the word *causing.*

We're not talking about the *importance* of good deeds. We're not talking about the *purpose* of good deeds. We're talking about the method of salvation. And when it comes to salvation, good deeds are not the cause. They are the result.

What is it that *causes* us to be saved? We know it's not our good deeds. Romans 3:20 says it clearly. "By the deeds of the law there shall no flesh be justified in his sight." *Jesus* is the One who saves us, and we are saved by accepting Him. "There is none other name under heaven given among men, whereby we must be saved." Acts 4:12.

The focus of our attention must not be on our deeds, whether those deeds are good or bad. In seeking for salvation, we are to focus on Jesus, and by beholding Him we become changed into His image. Any time we look to ourselves we will fail. Either we will see our sinfulness and become discouraged, or we will see our good behavior and become proud. It's a dead-end street either way. Only in looking to Jesus are we secure.

Paul was vehement on the subject of salvation by faith in Christ alone. But he wasn't against good works. He had been one of the best behaved persons in town. He talks about it in Philippians 3 and says, "If anybody has reason to boast of good works, I'll match my track record with his!" Yet in the end, he counted it all as loss when compared to the righteousness of Christ. "Judged by the letter of the law as men apply it to the outward life, he had abstained from sin; but when he looked into the depths of its holy precepts, and saw himself as God saw him, he bowed in humiliation and confessed his guilt."—*Steps to Christ,* pp. 29, 30.

One time I was discussing this thesis with a group of ministers. When we talked about the first half, that our good deeds have nothing to do with *causing* us to be saved, there was agreement all around. But when we came to the second half, that our bad deeds have nothing to do with *causing* us to be lost, some of them became uncomfortable.

But let me ask you, if the first is true, is not the second true as well? Aren't the two parts simply restating the same truth? Our salvation is based on our continuing acceptance of Jesus and His sacrifice for us, through a daily relationship with Him. It is not based on behavior. Salvation goes deeper than behavior. *And so does loss of salvation!* Behavior is not the dividing line for determining one's eternal destiny.

If you are saved at last, it will be because of what you have done in relationship to Jesus as your Saviour. Good deeds will undoubtedly be present, but they are not what *caused* your salvation. In the same way, if you are lost in the end, it will be because you left Jesus on the outside of your heart, knocking in vain for an entrance. Bad deeds may be present, but they will be the result, not the cause. God does not judge by the outward actions, but by the heart. Out of the heart are the issues of life. See 1 Samuel 16:7; Proverbs 4:23.

Thesis 8

Everyone is born sinful (or self-centered) because everyone is born separated from God.

As human beings, we have at least two things in common. First, we have been born. Second, we were born sinful. Our sin problem began at the point of birth, for we were born separated from God.

Sometimes people have trouble with this truth. They look at a newborn baby and say, "How can such a tiny, helpless person be sinful?" But few people have trouble accepting the fact that a newborn baby is self-centered! Never mind if mother is tired or father has to work tomorrow. If baby wants to be fed or cleaned up or entertained, he has ways of letting it be known. A baby is completely self-centered.

Being born into this world is a tragic experience! "The inheritance of children is that of sin. Sin has separated them from God."—*Child Guidance,* p. 475. Because of Adam's sin, his posterity were born with inherent propensities of disobedience. See Ellen G. White Comments, *S.D.A. Bible Commentary,* vol. 5, p. 1128.

In the first seven theses we have been dealing with the subject of righteousness. Since the opposite of righteousness is sin, that seems to be the next logical subject to consider. A clear understanding of righteousness and sin is essential to any study of the subject of salvation by faith. How you handle these two topics can be the crack in the sidewalk that becomes the Grand Canyon later on.

Our study on righteousness so far might be summed up by saying that righteousness comes through relationship with

Jesus; it is not based on behavior. If that is true, then we must also define sin as something more than behavior. We are sinful by birth; we are sinful by nature. It is our natures that are evil; our evil deeds are only the result.

Paul says in Ephesians 2:3 that we are by nature the children of wrath. Psalm 58:3 says, "The wicked are estranged from the womb: they go astray as soon as they be born." And in case you're not sure whom to include among the "wicked," remember Romans 3:10, "There are none righteous, no, not one."

A scorpion wanted to cross the river, so the story goes. He found a frog along the riverbank and asked for a ride on his back.

"Oh no," said the frog. "If I were to let you crawl up on my back, you would sting me, and I would die."

"Why would I do that?" asked the scorpion. "If I stung you and you died, then we would both drown, and I would never make it across the river."

Well, the scorpion's argument made sense to the frog, so he allowed the scorpion to climb on his back, and he began to swim across the river.

About halfway across, the scorpion stung him. As the frog croaked his last, he said, "Why did you do that? Now we'll both die!"

The scorpion replied sadly, "I know, but I couldn't help it. It is my nature."

This is the dilemma of the human race. Our natures are fallen. We cannot help ourselves. Even as we realize that we are destroying ourselves, we find that we are helpless to stop sinning, for it is our natures that are evil. "The result of eating of the tree of knowledge of good and evil is manifest in every man's experience. There is in his nature a bent to evil, a force which, unaided, he cannot resist."—*Education,* p. 29. Because of Adam's sin, "our natures are fallen and we cannot make ourselves righteous."—*Steps to Christ,* p. 62.

Because our sin problem goes deeper than simply doing wrong things, because we are sinful by nature from the moment we are born into this world of sin, then the answer to the problem of sin must go deeper than behavior. God proposes to

start all over again. He offers us a new birth, with an altogether new nature.

Jesus explained to Nicodemus in His midnight sermon to
that one-soul audience that unless there is a new birth, we have
no hope of ever seeing the kingdom of heaven. The first birth is
no good for eternal life—a second birth must follow. The good
news of salvation is that because of Jesus we can receive new
natures, and by sharing His divine nature, we can escape the
corruption of the sinful world into which we were born.

Thesis 9

God does not hold us accountable for being born sinful.

One day in southern California, a highway patrol officer pulled me over to the side of the road. That particular stretch of roadway happened to be under construction, which was the cause of the difficulty. I had been driving in the wrong lane, but didn't realize it was the wrong lane, because the lane markings were covered with dirt. Although I knew the law about driving in my own lane, I didn't realize I was breaking it at that time.

The officer who gave me the ticket was of the opinion that ignorance is no excuse. But I thought it was a very good excuse! So instead of paying the fine, I went in to plead my case in court. Fortunately, the judge saw things my way and canceled the ticket.

Do you think the judge was right, or the traffic officer? Do you think ignorance of transgression is a legitimate excuse, or not? How does God look at our ignorance, in terms of holding us accountable for breaking His law?

We could study several Bible passages to discover the answer to this question. Ezekiel 18:20 says, "The soul that sinneth, it shall die. The son shall not bear the iniquity of the father, neither shall the father bear the iniquity of the son: the righteousness of the righteous shall be upon him, and the wickedness of the wicked shall be upon him." In John 15:22, Jesus said, "If I had not come and spoken unto them, they had not had sin: but now they have no cloke for their sin." Again in John 9:41, "Jesus said unto them, If ye were blind, ye should have no sin: but now ye say, We see; therefore your sin remaineth."

Have you ever wondered why it took so many years before Jerusalem was destroyed after Jesus had come and spoken to the Jewish nation, leaving them without excuse? Why didn't fire come down from heaven the morning after the resurrection and destroy those who had murdered the Son of God?

The book *The Great Controversy* gives two reasons: First, not everyone had heard, even of the adults. Second, the children. "There were still many among the Jews who were ignorant of the character and the work of Christ. And the children had not enjoyed the opportunities or received the light which their parents had spurned. Through the preaching of the apostles and their associates, God would cause light to shine upon them; they would be permitted to see how prophecy had been fulfilled, not only in the birth and life of Christ, but in His death and resurrection. The children were not condemned for the sins of the parents; but when, with a knowledge of all the light given to their parents, the children rejected the additional light granted to themselves, they became partakers of the parents' sins, and filled up the measure of their iniquity."—Pages 27, 28.

Isn't it good news that the Judge of all the earth takes our ignorance of His law into consideration before pronouncing sentence upon us? Even though we are sinful by birth, He does not hold us accountable for our condition until we have had sufficient light and opportunity for repentance.

We have at least three problems with sin in this world. The first is the problem of the sinful nature with which we were born. The second is the problem of our sinful track record, our past sins which we have committed. The third is the problem of our present sinning. Sometimes people get the idea that if we were to stop our present sinning, and never sin or fall or fail again, that we would no longer need Jesus. But for as long as we live here, we will still need His justifying grace to cover our sinful past and our sinful nature.

On the other hand, some have believed that something needs to be done to atone for our sinful natures and, believing that we are sinful by birth, they have decided it is necessary to baptize infants in order to take care of that problem. Augustine taught what is sometimes called the doctrine of original sin, although it would have been more accurate to call it "original guilt." He believed in the sinful condition of man by birth—and he also believed that we are held accountable for that condition.

But God never holds any of us accountable for our sin—whether it is our sinful nature or our sins of the past or our present sinning—until we understand two things: First, that it is sin, and second, what to do about it. Only then does accountability begin.

God is not in the business of trying to see how many people He can keep out of heaven. Instead, because of His great love, He is doing everything a God of love can do to make it possible for each one to be there. The solution for the sinful nature, the sinful past, the present sinning, is provided for through His grace.

Thesis 10

We sin because we are sinful. We are not sinful because we sin.

A group of medical students were assigned a cadaver to study for their medical course. They gathered together in the room where the cadaver lay and discussed the problem before them.

"He looks awfully pale," said the first student.

"And he just lies there, doing nothing," added the second.

"I'm quite sure he's not getting enough exercise to stay healthy," observed the third.

"I think our first objective should be to get him up and around, to help get his circulation going," concluded the fourth. So they began trying to convince the cadaver to start moving about, but the cadaver just stayed on the table, cold and quiet, no matter what they said or did.

Now this is a parable! You have guessed that already! But using this somewhat gruesome analogy, let's restate thesis 10: "A cadaver lies on the table because he is dead. He is not dead because he lies on the table." The behavior that is typical of a corpse comes as a result of being dead—it is not the cause of death.

Spiritually, we are all born dead. Paul talks in Ephesians 2:1 of being "dead in trespasses and sins." The sinful deeds which sinful people commit are only the result of that condition, not the cause.

I'm not trying to say that sinning isn't sinful! But I am saying that sinning isn't what makes us sinful. If you could stop all sinful behavior right now, would that make you righteous? No, it would only make you well-behaved.

The Desire of Ages, page 21, says, "Sin originated in self-seeking." Think about that for a few minutes. Lucifer had been honored above all the angels of heaven. He was the highest of all created beings. But instead of continuing to seek after God, instead of seeking fellowship with Him, instead of seeking God's glory and honor as the highest goal, Lucifer began seeking his own glory. Sin didn't begin with Lucifer stealing apples off the tree of life. It began with self-seeking and glorifying the creature instead of the Creator.

It's a law of the universe that it is impossible to seek God's glory and our own glory at the same time. The first of the three angels in Revelation 14 comes with a message to every nation, and kindred, and tongue, and people. "Fear God, and give glory to him."—Verse 7. The work of the gospel has no room for the glory of man. Justification by faith "is the work of God in laying the glory of man in the dust, and doing for man that which is not in his power to do for himself."—*Testimonies to Ministers,* p. 456. Worshiping ourselves instead of God is the cause of all the sins that follow.

A strong-willed person may be able to control his behavior. But not even the strongest can change his sinful condition. "It is impossible for us, of ourselves, to escape from the pit of sin in which we are sunken. Our hearts are evil, and we cannot change them."—*Steps to Christ,* p. 18.

Any external change that we accomplish, apart from Christ, only results in our own glory coming to the top, and the glory of God going to the dust. And we end up farther than ever from the life in Christ that is offered through relationship and fellowship with Him.

A corpse can be washed and groomed and dressed in the finest clothes. It may not be guilty of doing even one wrong thing. It can even be taken to church. But it is still a corpse! Only new life from within, given by God, can bring about the change from death to life. That new life is received through relationship with Him. "The law of the Spirit of life in Christ Jesus hath made me free from the law of sin and death." Romans 8:2.

Thesis 11

Sin (singular)—living apart from God, results in sins (plural)—doing wrong things.

There is a difference between sin singular, living life apart from God, and sins plural, doing wrong things. Living apart from God is the basis of sin; the wrong deeds that we often call *sin* are only the result of our sinful condition.

Sometimes we get it backward. We think that doing wrong things is what separates us from God. But the truth is that separation from God is what leads us to do wrong things. Sin singular leads to sins plural.

Let's look at Solomon. Evidently he started out his reign with his heart perfect toward God. But as the years passed, a change came. "For it came to pass, when Solomon was old, that his wives turned away his heart after other gods: and his heart was not perfect with the Lord his God, as was the heart of David his father." 1 Kings 11:4.

What happened to Solomon? Did he begin doing wrong things, and persist in doing wrong things, until his heart was no longer perfect? No, it was the other way around. You find this description of his downfall in the Ellen G. White Comments, *S.D.A. Bible Commentary,* volume 2, page 1031: "All the sins and excesses of Solomon can be traced to his great mistake in ceasing to rely upon God for wisdom, and to walk in humility before Him."

The same was true of Eve. Some have thought she fell because she ate the apple—when the truth is that she ate the apple because she fell. At some point before she reached and took the fruit, she had come around to distrusting God and relying instead on herself. The act that followed was only the result.

It may take time for someone who is living apart from God to come to the place of open sinning. It took time for Solomon. It may also take time for someone who is seeking God and a relationship with Him to experience unbroken victory. It is possible to be seeking God and still to be growing in terms of behavior. But in the end, the condition of the heart toward God is the deciding factor for the outward life as well as for the inner.

"If sin (living life apart from God) is the cause of sins (doing wrong things), then where do the sins come from when we *are* seeking a relationship with God day by day?"

The Desire of Ages, page 668, answers that question in one sentence: "When we know God as it is our privilege to know Him, our life will be a life of continual obedience."

Even when we are seeking to know Him day by day, we may not yet know Him as it is our privilege to know Him. Thus there may be times when we take our eyes off Him for the moment. There may be times when we cease to depend upon Him and depend upon ourselves once again. And when we do, we will fail. But as we continue to seek to know Him, He will lead us to the point of trusting Him all of the time, so that our behavior will be right as well.

Thesis 12

Whoever lives life apart from God is living in sin.

If the real issue in sin lies in the area of relationship, rather than behavior, then anyone who lives life apart from God is living in sin. In fact, even the "good" deeds that are done apart from a faith relationship with God are sin. "Whatsoever is not of faith is sin." Romans 14:23. And when Jesus describes the work of the Holy Spirit to convict of sin, He says, "Of sin, because they believe not on me." John 16:9. As we try to grapple with this truth, let's consider the widow's lawn.

Suppose a widow lives across the street from my house, and every Sunday afternoon I mow her lawn. Is that a good deed or a bad deed? Well, it's probably a good deed as far as my neighbor is concerned. But what about my own heart? This thesis would insist that even mowing the widow's lawn would be sinful if I am living apart from God.

An atheist might decide to mow the neighbor's lawn. Would that make him a Christian? Someone who is simply a good church member, who wouldn't think of doing anything wrong, but who has no time for personal prayer and study and communion with God day by day, might mow the widow's lawn. But if the action is done apart from a vital relationship with God, the heart is wrong, and thus the action becomes sinful for him as well.

For instance, I might be mowing the widow's lawn because I want the neighbors to think I'm a good person. I might be mowing the widow's lawn because I am trying to atone for some past sin in my life. I might be mowing the widow's lawn because I've heard she has a good bit put away, and I'm hoping she will remember me in her will. Apart from God, my motives will be selfish, and any action I perform, good or bad externally, will be sinful.

It is possible for the most pleasing external appearance to cloak the worst kind of sin. For centuries, the universe has been amazed that often the weakest and most faltering end up the closest to God, while the strongest and best-behaved reject Him completely.

From among the disciples, the one who would have been voted most likely to succeed turned out to be the one who betrayed Jesus. The religious leaders of His day turned Him down and crucified Him, while the publicans and harlots and thieves became His steadfast followers. "The tempter often works most successfully through those who are least suspected of being under his control. . . . Many a man of cultured intellect and pleasant manners, who would not stoop to what is commonly regarded as an immoral act, is but a polished instrument in the hands of Satan."—*The Great Controversy,* p. 509. And *Steps to Christ,* page 58, tells us, "The love of influence and the desire for the esteem of others may produce a well-ordered life. Self-respect may lead us to avoid the appearance of evil. A selfish heart may perform generous actions."

If the heart is sinful, a well-ordered life can be an even greater deception. Which is more dangerous: a dark brown bottle under the sink, with skull and crossbones painted on it, and poison on the inside? Or a bottle in the refrigerator marked "7-Up," with poison on the inside?

Are you living in sin today? It makes little difference whether you are weak and faltering or whether you are a Pharisee of the Pharisees, like Paul before he met Jesus on the Damascus Road. The way to freedom from sin—whether that sin is manifested in "good" behavior or "bad" behavior—is to come to Jesus for salvation, and keep coming to Him. It is only Jesus who can lead us from sin to righteousness.

Thesis 13

The best definition for faith is trust. Trust is depending upon another.

Perhaps you have heard the story of the tightrope walker who was crossing Niagara Falls. After he had held the crowds spellbound with his daring, he asked, "How many of you believe I could cross the tightrope again, this time pushing a wheelbarrow with someone riding in it?"

The crowds applauded. They were sure he could do it. But then he said, "Who will volunteer to ride the wheelbarrow?"

There was a vast silence. The audience had just been reminded of the vital difference between belief and trust! It's one thing to believe that the wheelbarrow would make it safely across the chasm. It's quite another thing to put your own life on the line.

James 2:19 draws the same distinction: "Thou believest that there is one God; thou doest well: the devils also believe, and tremble." In order to have saving faith, you need more than simple mental assent. Even the devils have that much, and they tremble as a result. The devils believe—but they don't trust. And that is the crucial difference.

Three words describe the dependent relationship of the Christian to God: *faith, belief,* and *trust.* In modern usage, *belief* often carries with it the idea of only a mental assent. *Faith* is sometimes confused with positive thinking. But the word *trust* probably comes the closest to describing the biblical dependence upon God. Wherever you find the word *belief* or *faith* in Scripture, you can substitute the word *trust,* and perhaps understand a new dimension to familiar words. For instance, "Believe on the Lord Jesus Christ, and thou shalt be saved" (Acts 16:31), would read, *"Trust* the Lord Jesus Christ, and thou shalt be saved."

Selected Messages, book 1, page 389, says, "Faith includes not only belief but trust." And *Education,* page 253: "Faith is trusting God."

Faith is depending upon Another. It is probably the closest word to *surrender* to be found in the Bible, for it carries with it the idea of giving up your life into God's control.

High achievers don't like the idea of dependence. It can be frightening to think of placing yourself under the control of another. It can be a blow to human pride and self-sufficiency to allow someone else to call the shots. But "without faith it is impossible to please him" (Hebrews 11:6)—or, "without *trust* it is impossible to please him." Only when we give up our own will and way, and trust wholly in His power to save, can God accomplish His purpose in our lives.

> As children bring their broken toys
>   With tears, for us to mend,
> I brought my broken dreams to God
>   Because He was my Friend.
>
> But then, instead of leaving Him
>   In peace, to work alone
> I stayed around and tried to help
>   Through ways that were my own.
>
> At last I snatched them back and cried,
>   "How can you be so slow?"
> "My child," He said, "What could I do?
>   You never did let go."

Genuine faith, or trust, lets go. It depends completely. It is vulnerable. Human reasoning and understanding and logic can only go so far, and then we must step out into that which cannot be proved except by experience. Theologians have sometimes referred to this truth as the "leap of faith."

But trust in God is not a leap in the dark. He has given us enough evidence on which to base our trust in Him.

In Matthew 15 we find the story of the Syro-Phoenician woman. She came seeking Jesus, who had walked 50 miles out of His way so that her search would be rewarded. To find Him walking down the dusty roads of her own country must have encouraged her to believe. But when she brought her request to Him, He appeared to ignore her. She persisted, and He seemed to insult her. Yet there was enough evidence in His look and tone and manner to encourage her to trust Him in spite of appearances, and she persisted until her faith was rewarded. The answer came as she continued to depend upon Him.

Thesis 14

Knowing God results in trusting God. If you don't know Him, you won't trust Him. If you don't trust Him, you don't know Him.

Only two things are necessary in order to trust someone. First, you must find someone who is trustworthy. Second, you must get to know him. The reverse is also true. In order to distrust someone, all you need is to find someone who is not trustworthy—and then get to know him.

One summer while I was in academy I worked in a service station and learned to distrust service stations! The people I worked with that summer had many ways to take advantage of unwary customers. They would twist a fan belt in a way that would break it—and then take it to the customer and say, "Look, I discovered that your fanbelt is broken. Lucky I noticed it, huh?" Then they would collect the commission on the sale of a new fan belt. They would "change" the oil in one car by refilling it with oil removed from another car and thus charge double for the oil. They were not trustworthy, and I got to know them. Since then, I have been suspicious of service station attendants.

One time I stopped for gas. The man came to my window and held up a broken fan belt. I said, "You broke it; you replace it."

He acted shocked. "What do you mean?"

I said, "I used to work in a filling station."

"Oh."

And he replaced my fanbelt with no charge.

Now it is entirely possible that somewhere in this world there are honest filling station attendants. But in order for me to trust one of them ever again, I would have to know him very well. A casual relationship would not be enough. Not only would he have to be trustworthy, but I would have to take the time to get to know him well enough to trust him.

The Bible says that God is trustworthy. But you will never really trust Him until you get to know Him for yourself. We have already noticed the one-liner from *The Desire of Ages,* page 668, "When we know God as it is our privilege to know Him, our life will be a life of continual obedience." Add to that a line from *Steps to Christ,* page 61: "Obedience is the fruit of faith." If you must know God in order to obey, and if obedience comes from faith, then you must know God in order to have faith or trust in Him.

Sometimes we forget this truth, and we become involved in fighting sin and the devil. We try hard to obey, and we fall and fail time and time again. It is true that we are called to a fight—but it is essential to become involved in the right fight. "Fight the good fight of faith," says 1 Timothy 6:12. How do we fight the good fight of faith? By putting forth the necessary effort to get to know God so that we will trust in Him.

How do we get to know God? The same way we get to know anybody else. In order to get acquainted with anyone, three things are necessary. First, talk to them. Second, listen to them talk to you. And third, go places and do things together. Those are the ingredients of communication.

We talk to God through prayer. We listen to Him speak to us through His Word. And we go places and do things with Him by becoming involved in Christian service, witness, and outreach.

Sometimes people stumble over the idea of having a relationship with someone they can't see. One time a man came to H. M. S. Richards and said, "I don't believe in God."

"Why?" Richards asked.

The man replied, "Because I can't see Him."

Richards said, "I don't believe you have a brain."

"Why?"

"Because I can't see it."

We take advantage of many things we can't see. How long has it been since you saw electricity? Have you ever seen a radio wave? Unless you live in southern California, you can't see the air you breathe! We can't see the wind. We can't see germs and bacteria. We can't see that mysterious thing called "life." But we can see the results of all of the above!

Even though we cannot see God or hear His voice with our human equipment, we can still see the working of His power; and by taking advantage of the avenues of communication that He has given to us, we can come to know Him. It's in knowing Him that we learn to trust Him, for He is worthy of our trust.

Thesis 15

Faith is a fruit of the Spirit, not a fruit of the person. It is not something we work on, or work up.

If you are interested in producing anything from apples to zucchini, where do you start? Have you ever worked in a garden or orchard? Do you know how it's done? It doesn't take very much of a "green thumb" to recognize that certain things "cause" and other things "result." And if you wish to be successful in your garden or orchard, you don't put your effort on results, isn't that right?

What a blessing it would be if we could have the difference between cause and result as clear in our minds when it comes to spiritual growth. How many of us have wasted years and great effort trying to produce results—working on results! Paul lists the fruits seen in the Christian life. And notice that they are fruits of the Spirit, not fruits of the person. "The fruit of the Spirit is love, joy, peace, longsuffering, gentleness, goodness, *faith,* meekness, temperance: against such there is no law." Galatians 5:22, 23.

Scripture always presents faith as a fruit, or gift, or result. It is never our work. Romans 12:3 says that God has given to every one the measure of faith. Romans 10:17 says that faith comes by hearing, and hearing by the word of God. Faith always comes as a result of something else. You cannot work to produce it. You don't work on fruit. Instead, you put your effort toward that which produces the fruit. You don't work for a gift. You put your effort toward coming into the presence of the Giver and accepting the gift provided. "No man can create faith. The Spirit operating upon and enlightening the human mind, creates faith in God."—Ellen G. White Comments, *S.D.A. Bible Commentary,* vol. 7, p. 940.

It's easy to confuse faith with feeling, to try to work up faith by working up feeling. When do you find it easier to believe that God is going to answer your prayers? Is it when you feel that He's going to? Or is it when you feel sure that He isn't? When do you have more faith in God's promise to forgive the sins you have confessed to Him? Is it when you feel forgiven, or when you feel forsaken? Does your faith seem strong when things are going along smoothly, or when the roof has caved in and you are faced with trials and affliction?

But we are told that "feeling is not faith; the two are distinct."—*Early Writings,* p. 72. And this becomes another argument why we can never work on our faith. It is possible to work on your feelings. You can hear the right kind of music; you can be swayed by the eloquence of someone else who is trying to whip up some enthusiasm; you can be affected by the right lights or the spirit of the people around you. By working the crowds in the right way, it is possible to work up tremendous feeling. But after the lights are turned out and the masses return to their homes and you are left alone, what happens? You can end up feeling worse than before. Have you ever had it happen? Millions in our world today live from one emotional high to another, spending their life forces in a mad search for something to lift their spirits and help them forget that the last thing they tried didn't last.

The enemy has so successfully controlled the world on this basis that he still uses it as one of his best tools within the church. When someone makes the decision to come to Jesus to find the lasting happiness that He has to offer, the enemy comes and says, "You want to come to Jesus? Well, you'd better fix your life up so He will accept you." He gets that person working on results and keeps him from Jesus while he tries in vain to become righteous on his own. But then he hears about righteousness by faith. It sounds good. And as he determines to accept it, the enemy comes in with another ploy. He says, "That's right, righteousness comes by faith. Don't work on your righteousness; work on your faith." And that can be simply another barrier between the sinner and the Saviour.

The truth is that you don't work on your righteousness—nor do you work on faith. Both are gifts. Both are fruit. Both come as a result of knowing Jesus. And knowing Jesus comes as a result of spending time in communion and fellowship and relationship with Him. If you will come to Him, He will give you the genuine faith that you need. The first byproduct of seeking Jesus is genuine faith. Righteousness is the second.

Thesis 16

Positive thinking does not produce genuine faith, but faith will produce positive thinking.

Huss and Jerome were heores of the Reformation years. They worked in Bohemia, and their witness preceded that of Martin Luther in Germany. The writing of Wycliffe influenced both men. Not long after John Huss began to preach the gospel with great power, he was joined by Jerome, who had been in England.

As the preaching of John Huss became more widely known, he was summoned to Constance to give an account of his teachings. Huss was given a safe-conduct, but after his hearing he was thrown into prison anyway. Offered the opportunity to recant, he refused, and before many weeks had passed, he was burned at the stake. His persecutors scattered his ashes in the Rhine River and hoped in vain that they had silenced his voice.

When Jerome heard that his friend was in peril, he hurried to Constance, not waiting even for the safe-conduct that had proved so ineffective for John Huss. Upon his arrival, he, too, was thrown into prison and kept there for many months. His courage failed, and he accepted the opportunity to recant.

Then he discovered an amazing thing. There is something worse than being burned at the stake! And that is *not* to be burned at the stake—to live with the remorse of having denied the Lord. Jerome recanted his recantation and went singing to his death. When the executioner stepped behind him to kindle the flames, he cried, "Come forward boldly; apply the fire before my face. Had I been afraid, I should not be here."

The story of Huss and Jerome has much to teach us about

genuine faith. There is a pseudo-faith, popular today in the world and in the church, which is not faith at all but positive thinking. It would lead you to believe that faith consists of just believing that what you want is going to happen, that if you can find anything in Scripture that looks like a promise, you can claim it for your own. Frank Sinatra sings of this "positive thinking" in his song "I Did It My Way." Even within our own church, you can find the positive-thinking version of faith, proclaiming, "You can do it."

But the Bible's position is that not every promise is for you at this time and under these circumstances. If claiming promises is all that we need for deliverance, then Huss and Jerome blew it. Isaiah 43:2 has a wonderful promise they could have claimed: "When thou walkest through the fire, thou shalt not be burned; neither shall the flame kindle upon thee." But Huss and Jerome went to the stake—not because they lacked faith, but *because* of their faith.

Faith still trusts God even when things don't work out the way we want them to. It's easy to trust God when life is going smoothly. The real test of faith comes when our prayers seem unanswered. "The Lord would have you trust in His love and mercy amid clouds and darkness, as well as in the sunshine."— *Testimonies,* vol. 2, p. 274.

In our humanity, we can't help preferring the story of Daniel in the lions' den to the account of John the Baptist. We find it hard to understand when we read that "of all the gifts that heaven can bestow upon men, fellowship with Christ in His sufferings is the most weighty trust and the highest honor."— *The Ministry of Healing,* p. 478. We like the first part of Hebrews 11, the faith chapter, but we have trouble with the last part. Yet the last part is still there. Have you read it lately? After the glowing accounts of the deliverance God wrought for His people in various crises, it goes on to talk about the "others." Never forget the others! "Others were tortured, not accepting deliverance; that they might obtain a better resurrection: and others had trial of cruel mockings and scourgings, yea, moreover of bonds and imprisonment: they were stoned, they were sawn asunder, were tempted, were slain with the sword: they wandered about in sheepskins and goatskins; being destitute, afflicted, tormented; (of whom the world was not worthy:) they wandered in deserts, and in mountains, and in dens and caves of the earth. And these all, having obtained a good report through faith, received *not* the promise." Hebrews 11:35-39. (Emphasis supplied.)

The spiritual promises—for forgiveness of sin, for the Holy Spirit, for power to do His work—are always available. But the promises for temporal blessings, even for life itself, are given on occasion and withheld on occasion, as God's providence sees best. Are you willing to be among the "others" if God should call you to join with them in the deepest test of faith?

Thesis 17

Surrender is giving up on ourselves, not giving up our sins. Giving up our sins is the result of giving up on ourselves and seeking God.

Have you ever made any new year's resolutions? Some of us have made resolutions not only for the new year but for the first day of the month, the first day of the week, our birthday, the beginning of the school year, and whenever we moved to a new town!

Righteousness by resolution. "From now on, I will . . ." or, "From now on, I will not. . . ." Have you ever done it? Have you ever been frustrated to discover that it doesn't work?

We are talking about surrender in these next few theses, and one of the first basic principles of surrender is that if it does not include everything, it is not surrender at all. Surrender goes far deeper than giving up this or that bad habit. And even to say that we must surrender "everything" could be misleading. For surrender is not a matter of *things* at all. The only way we can give up everything is to give up on ourselves. The surrender of self is the basis of surrender.

When the Axis forces surrendered at the end of World War II, what did they surrender? Did they surrender just their guns and ammunition? Did they surrender just their tanks and hand grenades? Did they surrender just their uniforms and supplies? Or were they required to surrender themselves? And when they surrendered themselves, that automatically took care of the guns and bombs and tanks and all the rest.

Surrender cannot be done piecemeal. There is no such thing as partial surrender. It's no more possible to be partially surrendered than it is possible to be a little bit pregnant. Either you are, or you aren't. There is no middle ground.

If you study what the inspired writings to the church have to say you will find it described in all-or-nothing terms. Christ requires entire and unreserved surrender. See *Selected Messages,* bk. 1, p. 110. Unconditional surrender. See *Testimonies,* vol. 4, p. 120. Complete surrender. See *The Ministry of Healing,* p. 473. The list goes on and on.

When we talk about surrender, we are using a term that the King James Version of the Bible does not use, although the idea of surrender is found there. The King James Version uses the word *submit.* "Submit yourselves therefore to God" (James 4:7) is an example that gives a major clue to what is involved in complete or entire or unreserved surrender. As we have noticed, we don't just submit certain things. We submit ourselves. And in the process of submitting or surrendering self, whatever problems self has caused are automatically surrendered right along with the package. *Testimonies,* volume 9, pages 182, 183, puts it this way: "Each one will have a close struggle to overcome sin in his own heart. This is at times a very painful and discouraging work; because, as we see the deformities in our character, we keep looking at them, when we should look to Jesus and put on the robe of His righteousness. Everyone who enters the pearly gates of the city of God will enter there as a conqueror, and his greatest conquest will have been the conquest of self."

Surrender and faith are closely related. Only when we trust God and surrender, or give up ourselves, to Him do we depend upon Him instead of ourselves. By surrendering to Him, we give Him control. He can then work in us to will and to do of His good pleasure.

Thesis 18

Working to give up our sins can keep us from giving up on ourselves.

Let's suppose that you decide you want to give Bible studies to someone. You go to the pastor and ask if he can direct you to prospective members, and he says, "Yes, as a matter of fact I have two families who have requested Bible studies. You may choose which one you would prefer." And he describes them to you.

The first is a successful businessman in town. He and his wife are well thought of in the community. The wife does volunteer work at the town hospital, and the husband is involved in local politics. Their children are well-disciplined. Their home is immaculate. Neither of them smoke or drink. A few years ago they became interested in health and now not only go jogging five miles a day but are vegetarians as well. In fact, it was their interest in health that led them to inquire about Seventh-day Adventists.

The second family live downtown in a little apartment over a liquor store. The husband and wife—well, perhaps I should say the man and woman, for they only live together and are not legally married. Anyway, the couple are both unemployed; welfare provides their sole income. The man has served time in the county jail more than once for relatively minor offenses—petty theft, possession of narcotics, and similar charges. The woman is an alcoholic and severely overweight. She has three children, none of whom have the same father and none of whom are related to the current "man of the house." A few weeks ago the child protective agency removed the children from the home

65

temporarily, charging the parents with neglect and child abuse. This crisis brought about the initial contact with the Seventh-day Adventist Church, for the mother wants to be able to keep her children and says that they now realize they need God if they are going to get their lives together.

Which family would you like to become involved with? It's your choice! Which of these two families do you think has the greater potential for becoming good Christians, good Seventh-day Adventists?

I remember visiting the alcoholic husband of a church member. As we tried to talk, he stared up at me through bleary eyes and said, "I really admire the Adventists. It takes a strong man to be an Adventist."

Do you agree with that? Or can a weak person become a good Adventist? Might it be possible to fill the church with strong people who wouldn't think of doing anything wrong, but who never realize their need of Christ?

It makes no difference to the devil whether a person is lost inside or outside the church. And one of his detours to keep us from the genuine experience of surrender is to get us to work on our sins, to try hard to live good lives.

Working to give up your sins is a dead-end street whether you are strong or weak. If you are strong, your good behavior can become a barrier between you and the Saviour. If you are weak, you can become so discouraged and overwhelmed by your failures that you give up completely. "We are not to look at ourselves. The more we dwell upon our own imperfections, the less strength we shall have to overcome them."—Ellen White, *Review and Herald,* January 14, 1890.

The Jewish nation at the time of Christ demonstrated this principle. The Jewish church was full of strong people. It took a strong man to be a Pharisee! Yet it was the strong people who rejected Jesus and finally crucified Him.

The weak people in the Jewish nation were on the outside, condemned as great sinners. The leaders had excommunicated them long ago for their falling and sinning. They had given up hope of ever making it to the kingdom. Yet the weak people flocked around Jesus, accepted His offer of grace, and became

His most steadfast followers.

It looks pretty hopeless for the strong person, doesn't it? Shall we all go out and get drunk so that we can recognize our need? Or shall we all, strong or weak, realize once again that our behavior neither saves us nor causes us to be lost. All must come to Jesus for His salvation.

Are you a strong person? So was Paul. So was Nicodemus. Are you weak? So was Mary. So were Peter and Matthew. So was the demoniac. All of them had a common need, the need to give up on themselves and come to Jesus. All of them found that He accepted them when they came to Him.

He will accept you today as well.

Thesis 19

No one can crucify himself or bring himself to surrender. Someone else must do that for him.

Perhaps one of the hardest truths to accept in the area of surrender is that we can't do it! If we could work on surrender, we wouldn't have to surrender. If we could do something, then we wouldn't have to surrender. Because surrender, or giving up, is admitting that we can do nothing. Inevitably, therefore, the work of bringing us to the point of surrender must be the work of God. It is not something we can do for ourselves.

As we have noticed earlier, the devil has prepared sidetracks at every step for the one who becomes aware of his need of Christ and decides to come to Jesus. He says, "You are a sinner, and you have no righteousness. That's right—go to work on your righteousness." And we can spend futile days and years trying to produce righteousness by willpower.

Then we hear about the truth that righteousness comes only by faith, and the devil jumps in and says, "That's right, you need faith. Start working on your faith."

And after we come to understand that faith is a gift, not our own work, he meets us again at the last step in coming to Christ, surrender, and says, "OK, now what you need to do is to try hard to surrender."

Sometimes parents and teachers and ministers and other church leaders have unwittingly helped the devil in his campaign! Have you ever been to a meeting where a minister or a teacher invited you to work hard on surrender? Have you ever seen, perhaps, a little altar up front with a little fire going and slips of paper handed up and down the aisles? And you write the sin that you want to give up on the piece of paper and take it up and put it in the fire. Is that surrender?

Have you ever wondered how to rid yourself of some sin in your life and have someone tell you that all you have to do is give it up? And you try giving it up. You say the words. You say, "I give up my dishonesty," or "I give up my evil thoughts." You *pray* the words. But you find that dishonesty and evil thoughts are still with you.

The Bible uses the analogy of the crucifixion as a symbol of the experience of surrender. "I am crucified with Christ," Paul says. Galatians 2:20. Jesus used the symbol repeatedly, inviting His followers to take up their cross and follow Him. See Matthew 10:38; Luke 14:27; Mark 8:34. In fact, whenever Jesus spoke of the cross, He always referred to it as *our* cross, never His own.

Think for a minute about crucifixion. How was it accomplished? That's easy to remember, isn't it? How many times have we seen the artwork and heard about the nails and the wood? But notice one thing particularly. You cannot crucify yourself. Someone else has to do it for you.

If you want to kill yourself, you can do it any number of ways. You can put a gun to your head and pull the trigger. You can jump off the Golden Gate Bridge or the Empire State Building. You can take an overdose of sleeping pills, or lock yourself in your car in the garage with the motor running. People have tried all sorts of methods with greater or lesser success. But no one has ever yet been able to commit suicide by crucifying himself.

Christ's Object Lessons expresses it this way, "No man can empty himself of self. We can only consent for Christ to accomplish the work."—Page 159. How do we consent for Christ to do the work? It involves more than just saying or praying the words. "The lips may express a poverty of soul that the heart does not acknowledge. While speaking to God of poverty of spirit, the heart may be swelling with the conceit of its own superior humility and exalted righteousness. In one way only can a true knowledge of self be obtained. We must behold Christ."—*Ibid.*

As we make the choice to spend time day by day in beholding Christ, as we invite Him to do His work in our lives, He will lead us step by step to the point of surrender. Giving up is possible only when He has brought us up to that point.

Thesis 20

We are controlled by God or Satan. The only control we have is to choose who will control us.

Would you like to take a little quiz? Mark only one answer for each question!

1. Are you
   - A. a Republican?
   - B. a Democrat?
   - C. none of the above?

2. Are you
   - A. a millionaire?
   - B. a pauper?
   - C. none of the above?

3. Are you
   - A. a genius?
   - B. an imbecile?
   - C. none of the above?

4. Are you
   - A. beautiful?
   - B. ugly?
   - C. none of the above?

5. Are you
   - A. being controlled by God?
   - B. being controlled by Satan?

And right there, we have to break the pattern for our little quiz. You can occupy all kinds of middle ground in this world. You can be indifferent to politics, middle-class, averagely intelligent, moderately attractive. But when it comes to who controls your life, there is no middle ground. It's an all-or-nothing proposition.

"Know ye not, that to whom ye yield yourselves servants to obey, his servants ye are to whom ye obey; whether of sin unto death, or of obedience unto righteousness?" Romans 6:16. Two choices. Sin unto death. Or obedience unto righteousness. Those are the only choices. Jesus said it in Luke 11:23, "He that is not with me is against me."

The book *The Desire of Ages* contains four major references that explain this truth—pages 125, 258, 324, and 466. You may wish to read them in their entirety on your own, but I will quote from two of them here.

"Unless we do yield ourselves to the control of Christ, we shall be dominated by the wicked one. We must inevitably be under the control of the one or the other of the two great powers that are contending for the supremacy of the world. It is not necessary for us deliberately to choose the service of the kingdom of darkness in order to come under its dominion. We have only to neglect to ally ourselves with the kingdom of light."— *Ibid.*, p. 324.

"Every soul that refuses to give himself to God is under the control of another power. He is not his own. He may talk of freedom, but he is in the most abject slavery."—*Ibid.*, p. 466.

This idea sometimes makes people nervous. "But what about our individuality?" they ask. "If we are totally controlled by God, won't that do away with our power of choice? Won't we become puppets?"

Actually, it is refusing to come under God's control that makes us puppets and sacrifices our individuality! Because God's control brings with it the freedom at any time to choose to pull out. It is the enemy who holds fast those who are under his control, refusing to release them.

As human beings, we are instruments. Romans 6:13 says we can be instruments of righteousness unto God, or instruments of unrighteousness unto sin. We sing it: "Have thine own way, Lord! Have thine own way! Hold o'er my being absolute sway." But we still may refuse to accept it. Are you an instrument? An instrument is controlled by another. An ax isn't good or bad in itself. An ax can chop firewood to warm the house for the winter, or it can murder someone. It's who's controlling the instrument that decides. A violin can make either heavenly sounds or excruciating ones, depending on who controls it.

We too are instruments. Who is controlling us today?

SURRENDER

Thesis 21

The surrender of the will is the surrender of the power of choice, but we use our power of choice to surrender it. We give up our power of choice toward behavior; we keep our power of choice toward relationship.

Please get out your magnifying glass and join me in looking very closely at one page, page 47, in the book *Steps to Christ*.

"Many are inquiring, '*How* am I to make the surrender of myself to God?' You desire to give yourself to Him, but you are weak in moral power, in slavery to doubt, and controlled by the habits of your life of sin. Your promises and resolutions are like ropes of sand. You cannot control your thoughts, your impulses, your affections. The knowledge of your broken promises and forfeited pledges weakens your confidence in your own sincerity, and causes you to feel that God cannot accept you; but you need not despair."

The first time I read that, I said, "How did the author of *Steps to Christ* know me so well?" But the page had good news. It said, "You need not despair. What you need to understand is the true force of the will."—*Ibid.*

"That's right," I thought. "I don't have enough force to my will. I can't stay out of the cookie jar. I can't make myself go jogging. I can't control my temper. I need more will power." And I'd start in again with the promises and resolutions, made with ropes of sand, and end up right where I had started. It was so discouraging that before too many times, whenever I would come to page 47, I'd say, "Oh—that again!" And skip to page 49!

But the explanation is inherent in the context, if you take the time to really look at it. "What you need to understand is the true force of the will. This is the governing power in the nature of man, the power of decision, or of choice."

So what is the will? The power of choice. There is a vast difference between the will—the power of choice—and will power—self-discipline or backbone. So let's continue reading, and substitute "the power of choice," the synonym that the context gives for the word *will*.

"Everything depends on the right action of the will. [OK, substitute. Everything depends on the right action of the power of choice.] The power of choice God has given to men; it is theirs to exercise. You cannot change your heart, you cannot of yourself give to God its affections; but you can *choose* to serve Him. You can give Him your will. [You can give Him your power of choice.] He will then work in you to will and to do according to His good pleasure. Thus your whole nature will be brought under the control of the Spirit of Christ. . . .

"Many will be lost while hoping and desiring to be Christians. They do not come to the point of yielding the will to God. [They do not come to the point of yielding the power of choice to God.] . . .

"Through the right exercise of the will [power of choice], an entire change may be made in your life. By yielding up your will [power of choice] to Christ, you ally yourself with the power that is above all principalities and powers. You will have strength from above to hold you steadfast, and thus through constant surrender to God you will be enabled to live the new life, even the life of faith."—Pages 47, 48.

But it takes using your power of choice to give up your power of choice! It's the distinction between behavior and relationship once again. We give up our power of choice toward behavior. We keep our power of choice toward relationship. As we continue to choose to enter into a daily personal relationship with Christ, *He* works in us, to will and do of His good pleasure. We cannot bring ourselves to the point of giving up our will, another term for surrender. But we can consent for Christ to do the work, by placing ourselves in His hands as we seek a personal relationship with Him.

Thesis 22

The only *deliberate* effort in the Christian life is to seek God. Spontaneous effort toward other things will result.

Suppose that one Sunday morning you decide to rotate the tires on your Datsun. You get it up on jacks and manage to remove all four tires. Just then your wife calls you in for lunch.

Before you finish eating, your four-year-old daughter goes out to play in the front yard. Her ball rolls under the Datsun, and she crawls under the car to get it, knocking loose one of the jacks.

You hear her screams and look out the window by the table. You can see the car from where you sit and understand immediately what has happened. So you . . .

What *do* you do at that point? Do you lean back in your chair and say to your wife, "Looks like the car has fallen on Mary. Guess I'd better go out and jack it up again. But first, could you get me one more piece of that apple pie?"

Or do you rush to the front yard, exert superhuman strength, and lift the end of the car off your daughter so that she is freed?

Which would be easier for you to do? Wait—don't answer too quickly. Which is easier in terms of deliberate effort? To sit at the table and have a second piece of pie, or to lift a car—even if it *is* a Datsun? Which takes more energy? Which burns more calories? Which gives you more exercise?

On the other hand, if you love your child at all, which would be harder to do? There's no contest, is there? It may require superhuman strength to lift the end of the car so that your child can be saved, but it would require impossible effort to remain seated at the table!

79

The distinction between deliberate effort and spontaneous effort is an important one in understanding the effort involved in living the Christian life. Sometimes people get the idea when we talk about not fighting sin and the devil in our own strength, that we are talking about an effortless religion. There was a strange sect called Quietists in the last century, who believed that we should put forth no effort at all. We should just sit and rock—in fact, that would probably be too much. We should just sit. Whatever needs to be done, God Himself will take care of, apart from us.

But God never bestows salvation upon us apart from our effort. The problem we have so often had is misunderstanding where to direct our effort. This dilemma has often kept the theologians debating until midnight, but it is answered clearly in two texts that are a mini-course in righteousness by faith, as concise a statement on the subject of divine power versus human effort as you are ever likely to discover.

The two texts are John 15:5 and Philippians 4:13. The words of Jesus, "Without me ye can do nothing," and Paul's comment, "I can do all things through Christ." Put the two together. If without Christ we can do nothing, but with Him we can do all things, then what is left for us to do? Get with Him and stay with Him.

"All that man can possibly do toward his own salvation is to accept the invitation, 'Whosoever will, let him take the water of life freely.' "—*Selected Messages,* bk. 1, p. 343. And don't forget that the term *salvation* includes not only pardon for sin, but power for obedience, and heaven at last—justification, sanctification, and glorification.

How do we get with Christ? How do we take the water of life? "In this communion with Christ, through prayer and the study of the great and precious truths of His word, we shall as hungry souls be fed; as those that thirst, we shall be refreshed at the fountain of life."—*Thoughts From the Mount of Blessing,* p. 113.

For the parent, the deliberate effort that has been invested day by day in relationship with the child may have required hard work at times. But when a crisis comes, the necessary effort is wholly spontaneous. No parent who loves would stop to consider the energy required, but would rush to the aid of his child who is in trouble.

Thus it is for the Christian. All kinds of effort are required in the Christian life. But the one *deliberate* effort is to seek communion with God. Spontaneous effort toward the other things will surely result.

Thesis 23

Growing Christians experience on-again, off-again surrender. Sometimes they depend on God, sometimes on themselves.

The disciples walked along the road to Capernaum. Their footsteps grew slow, and still slower, until they had lagged almost out of sight behind Jesus. They were having a heated discussion among themselves and hardly noticed that Jesus was no longer with them—except for a quick glance now and then to be sure He was out of earshot.

The subject of their discussion was a favorite: Who was to be the greatest in the kingdom? On occasion they had gone so far as to include Jesus in these debates, hoping for some straight answer from Him that might settle the issue. But He had answered them only with a parable about little children, instead of giving each of them the clear job description for which they had hoped. Now they were embarrassed for Him to know they still argued the matter.

Nor would this be the last time the disciples became involved in this squabble, in spite of Jesus' repeated efforts to instruct them. They would listen to His words in the house at Capernaum that day. They would realize their error in seeking the highest place, the very sin of Lucifer in the beginning. But before long James and John would come, through their mother, with an out-and-out request for the highest places, on the right hand and on the left, and the disciples would be at it again. A little while later, Peter, James, and John would be included in the mysterious trip to the mountaintop, and the nine who were left behind would spend the night arguing about who was to be the greatest. Even the humiliation of being unable to cast out a demon the next morning was not enough to teach them their lesson. For in the upper room, the night before the crucifixion, they were again at swords' points, each one unwilling to concede the highest place and take the part of a servant.

The disciples were committing sin. They knew it was sin. Yet they kept doing it time and time and time again.

Who were these disciples? Well, they were men who had the benefit of three years spent in close relationship with Jesus. They associated with Him day by day. They were converted men, for Jesus told them when they returned from their missionary journey, rejoicing in the power given them over the demons, that they should rather rejoice because their names were written in heaven. See Luke 10:20. The book of life doesn't include the names of those who have never been converted. See John 3.

The story of the disciples is a disturbing story to some. It is as biblical as your Bible, and in fact the pattern of on-again, off-again doesn't begin or end with the disciples. Abraham, Jacob, Elijah, David, Mary and Martha, and even Paul, exhibit the same pattern, along with many others. It is disturbing, but it is reality. A reality that Scripture chronicles faithfully.

We have noticed earlier that there is no such thing as partial surrender. Surrender is either all or nothing. But there *is* the possibility of inconstant surrender. In fact, based on the biographies the Bible gives us, we might even go so far as to say that inconstant surrender is not just a possibility. More often than not, it took time and trial and error before the one who had surrendered to God learned to *stay* surrendered to Him all of the time, without wavering.

Thesis 72 will go into greater detail regarding this on-again, off-again pattern in the Christian life. But for now, let's cover just this much: suppose you find yourself in the disciples' shoes? Suppose you discover that one minute you're depending upon God and experiencing victory—and the next minute, you somehow begin depending on yourself and find that you have fallen and failed and sinned again. What do you do?

Here is instruction and encouragement for just such a person. "If one who daily communes with God errs from the path, if he turns a moment from looking steadfastly unto Jesus, it is not because he sins willfully; for when he sees his mistake, he turns again, and fastens his eyes upon Jesus, and the fact that he has erred, does not make him less dear to the heart of God."—Ellen White, *Review and Herald,* May 12, 1896.

Thesis 24

Conversion is the work of the Holy Spirit, which produces a change of attitude toward God and creates a new capacity for knowing God.

You can't choose your own birthday! Nobody yet has been able to do that. By the time we get here, our birthday has already been chosen. And, in spite of the progress in modern medical science, it's not easy to choose someone else's birthday either.

Conversion is called the new birth. It's the beginning of spiritual life. And just as in the physical life, you cannot choose your own spiritual birthday.

When my son was in the academy, I decided it was time for him to become converted. I sat him down one day, intending to do the job. It didn't work. We both ended up frustrated. I had forgotten the first principle in conversion—that it is the work of the Holy Spirit. We cannot convert ourselves, nor can we convert someone else. "This change can be brought about only by the effectual working of the Holy Spirit."—*The Desire of Ages,* p. 172.

Young people have often misunderstood what conversion really is. Some have looked for a Damascus Road experience, forgetting that even Paul needed three silent years in the desert of Arabia before he was ready to begin his public ministry. At the other extreme, others aren't sure whether they've been converted at all, but assume they must have been since they were raised within the church. Some have made a commitment to Christ, and when they have not found themselves miraculously changed in character the morning after the night before, they conclude they were not converted and wait for the next emotional appeal to try it again.

To find a definition for conversion, then, becomes extremely important. Conversion is a work of the Holy Spirit, and it produces a change of attitude toward God. When was the prodigal son converted? While he was in the pigpen. And where was the prodigal son immediately after his conversion? Still in the pigpen! Someone usually adds at that point, "But he didn't stay there long." That's true. But what changed at his conversion? It was his attitude. He still had a long way to go to reach his father's house, but his attitude toward his father underwent a major change. And that change of attitude prepared the way for the rest of the changes that followed.

Conversion creates a new capacity for knowing God. No one is able to eat or breathe for themselves until they are born. And while it is possible to hasten the process of conversion by placing yourself in an atmosphere of spiritual things, the attempt at a devotional life will be nothing but boring and hard work until you are born spiritually. First Corinthians 2:14 says, "The natural man receiveth not the things of the Spirit of God: for they are foolishness unto him: neither can he know them, because they are spiritually discerned."

One of the miracles that the Holy Spirit accomplishes at the time of conversion is to create a new capacity for knowing God. "In order to serve Him aright, we must be born of the divine Spirit. This will purify the heart and renew the mind, giving us a new capacity for knowing and loving God."—*The Desire of Ages,* p. 189.

It doesn't matter if you come from a background of atheists or genuine Christians, *you* must be born again in order to see the kingdom of heaven. Jesus said to Nicodemus in John 3:3, "Except a man be born again, he cannot see the kingdom of God."

And you can know whether or not you have been converted. It is true that conversions differ just as our human emotional machinery differs, but the experience of conversion is still distinctive. "Little by little, perhaps unconsciously to the receiver, impressions are made that tend to draw the soul to Christ.

These may be received through meditating upon Him, through reading the Scriptures, or through hearing the word from the living preacher. Suddenly, as the Spirit comes with more direct appeal, the soul gladly surrenders itself to Jesus."—*The Desire of Ages,* p. 172.

Has the "suddenly" happened to you as yet? Have you been depending on your good behavior, your position in the church, or your Christian heritage to insure you salvation?

Or have you been focusing on your weaknesses and mistakes and concluding on that basis that you have never been converted?

When you understand what conversion is, you can know whether or not you have been converted.

Thesis 25

Conversion leads to a changed life.

No drive-through window or fast-food chain offers the fruit of the Spirit. Spiritual growth takes time. Jesus' parable compared spiritual and physical development: "First the blade, then the ear, after that the full corn in the ear." Mark 4:28.

Just coming to Christ—apart from growing in Him—involves a process. The first step is a *desire* for something better. We may not even recognize this desire as having anything to do with God. We may simply desire a better car or better job or better grade point average. But God has placed within each heart a reaching out for something more.

The second step in coming to Christ is to gain a *knowledge* of what it is that's better. Through the Scripture, through the testimony of other Christians, through the working of the Holy Spirit upon the heart, we learn of the plan of salvation, God's answer to the emptiness of the human heart.

The third step in coming to Christ is the *conviction* that we are sinners. We are convicted of our condition—not merely of our sinful behavior. As we gain a knowledge of God's love, we realize how little we have valued it. We recognize that we have lived independently of Him. We see our desperate condition and realize our need of His salvation.

The fourth step in coming to Christ is the realization that we are *helpless* to do anything at all about our condition. Young people especially may teeter for years between steps 3 and 4, recognizing that they are sinners, but not yet admitting that they cannot help themselves out of their condition.

Finally, we come to the end of our own resources. When we see our helplessness, there is only one thing left to do. Give up. It's spelled S-U-R-R-E-N-D-E-R. As we have already noticed, we cannot bring ourselves to the point of giving up. But when God has brought us there, we ourselves make the choice to give up to Him.

Steps to Christ, page 18, describes the miracle of conversion, or the new birth: "The Saviour said, 'Except a man be born from above,' unless he shall receive a new heart, new desires, purposes, and motives, leading to a new life, 'he cannot see the kingdom of God.' "

Don't miss those words, *"leading to* a new life." It doesn't all happen overnight. Physical birth is a beginning. The new birth is a beginning. It is not a complete change of life and habit patterns overnight. But it *is* a complete change of direction.

We've already spent time looking at the disciples, who continued for three and a half years to struggle with some of the same problems before they finally experienced the breakthrough to victory. Jacob surrendered to God at Bethel, but it was twenty years before the crisis in his life by the brook Jabbok brought him to the end of his self-dependence. Mary came to Jesus seven times, seeking His prayers in her behalf to cast out the demons that controlled her life. It took time for her to understand how to stay surrendered to Him all of the time.

But for all of these, there was a common denominator. They were now seeking fellowship with Jesus instead of running from Him. Their direction had changed. They had a new capacity for knowing and loving God. Their attitude toward God had changed. And as they continued to seek Jesus, the process of growth and maturity did its work, and their lives were transformed.

The Ministry of Healing, page 454, tells us, "The precious graces of the Holy Spirit are not developed in a moment. Courage, fortitude, meekness, faith, unwavering trust in God's power to save, are acquired by the experience of years."

We will study more on the subject of temptation under Theses 80 to 84. But for now, notice just this much: Where does yielding to temptation begin? "Yielding to temptation begins in permitting the mind to waver, to be inconstant in your trust in God."—*Thoughts From the Mount of Blessing,* p. 92. And how long does it take to have unwavering trust in God? It doesn't happen overnight. It takes time.

Have you given yourself to God? Do you continue to come to Him day by day in fellowship and communion? And do you still find yourself inconstant in your trust in Him? Welcome to the club. Your new heart is *leading to* a new life. Are you willing to keep coming to Him, even if you find yourself slow in learning the lessons He would teach you? Are you willing to give God time?

Thesis 26

Conversion and repentance are continuing experiences, not once only.

One time a college student dropped by my office and said, "I made a decision to give my life to Christ last summer at a camp meeting, and this time I really thought I was converted. But within a few weeks, I was farther from God than ever. This has happened to me time and time again. What's wrong that my conversions never last?"

Conversion is not *supposed* to last longer than one day! This student's dilemma wasn't a problem of being converted too often—it was a problem of not being converted often enough!

We don't believe in once-converted, always-converted. If you are really converted today, you still need to be really converted tomorrow. Conversion must be a daily matter.

One summer I worked as a student colporter in the sandhills of Nebraska. I expected that the experience I had with God during the summer would continue right through the school year. But when the busy school schedule hit me and, surrounded by my friends, I no longer felt such a need to seek God, the high experience of the summer quickly faded. Spiritually, it turned out to be one of my worst school years.

Even the most spectacular manifestations of God's power quickly lose their power to influence us. It was true in the time of Christ. He had fed 5,000 men, plus women and children, from a few loaves and fishes. Heaven had seemed to come down to earth. The people were ready to crown Him king. You can read about it in John 6.

Just twenty-four hours later, when He refused their request

for new and greater miracles, the people were just as ready to turn away from Him in disgust. They had no patience to eat the mysterious Bread of Life of which He spoke. So many of them turned from Him that day that He finally asked His disciples, "Are you going away too?" Apparently His disciples were about the only ones left.

If you haven't discovered the necessity of daily conversion, it can be a major breakthrough in your life. *Thoughts From the Mount of Blessing,* page 101, makes this promise: "If you will seek the Lord and be converted every day . . . all your murmurings will be stilled, all your difficulties will be removed, all the perplexing problems that now confront you will be solved."

Conversion and repentance are closely linked together, and I've included repentance in this thesis as I make the transition into the theses concerning repentance. But repentance is not a once-in-a-lifetime experience. It, too, is to be a daily matter.

When I speak of repentance as a daily necessity, I'm not talking about repentance for wrong deeds. You have probably heard the story about the man who said to his pastor, "I've asked God to forgive me for this particular sin a thousand times."

And the pastor responded, "That's 999 times too many!"

I'm not campaigning for an endless recital of our faults and failings. God has promised that "if we confess our sins, he is faithful and just to forgive us our sins." 1 John 1:9. Instead I'm talking about repentance in the sense described in *The Acts of the Apostles,* page 561: "None of the apostles and prophets ever claimed to be without sin. Men who have lived the nearest to God, men who would sacrifice life itself rather than knowingly commit a wrong act, men whom God has honored with divine light and power, have confessed the sinfulness of their nature." This is the repentance which is needed daily, the repentance brought about by a renewed realization of our sinful condition which makes the grace of God a necessity. This is the repentance of which it is said, "At every advance step in our Christian experience our repentance will deepen."—*Ibid.*

Are you converted? Have you been converted *today?* Have you come to God for repentance *today?*

Thesis 27

Repentance is sorrow for sin and turning away from sins. Repentance is a gift. Therefore, sorrow for sin is a gift, and turning away from sins is a gift.

Early in my ministry, I found myself in a most uncomfortable position. I was not converted, and I didn't know how to become converted. I wasn't saved, and I didn't know how to get saved. And for one who is unconverted and unsaved the gospel ministry is the most uncomfortable place in the world to be!

Summer came. The time for camp meeting rolled around. As a new minister, one of my duties was to help pitch tents at the campground the week before the meetings began. The ministers assigned to this task got the first row of tents pitched, so they would have something to stand behind, and then they needed a rest! We weren't used to this kind of exercise! While we rested for a while between the rows of tents, we became involved in all sorts of theological discussions. We talked about where the Battle of Armageddon would be fought and whether or not angels' wings have feathers! I saw my opportunity.

Going up to one of the older ministers, I asked, "What do you tell someone who asks you how to be saved?" (That seemed a safe way to phrase it!)

He said, "I tell them to repent."

"What if they ask how to repent."

"Well, repentance is being sorry for your sins and turning away from them."

"OK, how do you turn away from your sins?"

"Why, you repent!"

97

I said, "Wait a minute. Are you telling me that the way to turn away from your sins is to turn away from your sins, and the way to repent is to repent?"

"Yes, that's right," he beamed, obviously pleased with my clear grasp of the subject.

The classic definition for repentance, found on page 23 of *Steps to Christ,* uses those very words. "Repentance includes sorrow for sin and a turning away from it." But the truth about repentance that I had missed is that repentance is a gift. It's not something we achieve; it's something we receive. That makes all the difference.

Acts 5:31 tells us that repentance is the gift of God. *Selected Messages,* book 1, page 353, says clearly, "Repentance, as well as forgiveness, is the gift of God through Christ." So any repentance that we try to work up on our own, any repentance that is self-generated, will inevitably fall short of the genuine article. We may be able to be sorry for the consequences of our evil deeds. We may regret the results of our life of sin. But unless we receive the repentance that is a gift from God, we will be unable to go any farther than that.

Sorrow for sin, sorrow for having lived life separated from God, can come only from God Himself. We cannot make ourselves sorry. Genuine sorrow for sin is a gift.

And turning away from sins is a gift as well. We don't turn away from sins in order to repent. We come to Jesus in order to repent! And Romans 2:4 says it is the goodness of God that leads us to repentance. We most fully recognize the evil of sin when we most fully realize the love of Jesus. As we study the life of Jesus, as we contemplate His sacrifice for us upon the cross, our hearts are broken, and we experience genuine repentance. Sin no longer looks attractive. When our hearts are changed, our actions are changed, and we receive the gift of repentance that does not need to be repented of. Our part is only, always, to come to Him.

Thesis 28

We do not change our lives in order to come to Christ. We come to Him just as we are, and He changes our lives.

One day a nurse stopped by my office. She said, "I'm sick and tired of my life. I know I need God, and I'd like to come to Him. Will you please help me?"

Well, that's just the kind of opportunity any preacher is excited about. So I said, "Of course! All you have to do is come to Him in prayer and ask Him to forgive your sin and take control of your life. We can do that right now."

"No," she said, "Wait a minute. I have plans for this weekend." She went on to tell me about her plans. She was going out of town with someone else's husband. She wanted to come to Christ, but she didn't want to change her plans for the weekend. And it was Thursday afternoon.

I said, "You can come to Christ just as you are. You don't have to change your plans for the weekend in order to come to Christ. You come to Christ just as your are, and *He* will deal with your plans."

She said, "You don't really believe that!"

Now let me ask you. Who was right? Did she have to change her plans for the weekend before she could come to Christ? Or would He accept her *with* her plans for the weekend? Which do you believe?

Jeremiah 3:13 says, "Only acknowledge thine iniquity, that thou hast transgressed against the Lord thy God." Well, this young nurse had done that much. She admitted that her plans for the weekend were wrong. But she still wasn't willing to give them up.

How is repentance accomplished? Do we come to Christ in order to repent, or do we repent in order to come to Christ? In the area of repentance, we have often found ourselves in the shoes of the man whose horn on his car wouldn't work. So he went to the garage for repairs, and on the door of the garage was a sign which read, "Honk for service."

The chapter on repentance in *Steps to Christ* explains the way out of this apparent dilemma. It says, "Just here is a point on which many err, and hence they fail of receiving the help that Christ desires to give them. They think they cannot come to Christ unless they first repent, and that repentance prepares for the forgiveness of their sins. It is true that repentance does precede the forgiveness of sins; for it is only the broken and contrite heart that will feel the need of a Saviour. But must the sinner wait till he has repented before he can come to Jesus? Is repentance to be made an obstacle between the sinner and the Saviour?"—Page 26.

The answer to that question comes on the same page, "We can no more repent without the Spirit of Christ to awaken the conscience than we can be pardoned without Christ." Repentance isn't something we do; it's a gift. In order to receive a gift, we must first come into the presence of the Giver.

So if you are a young nurse on a Thursday afternoon, longing for something better in your life, but unable to change your plans for the weekend, you can come to Christ just as you are. You will never be able to change your life of sin apart from Him. But when you come to Him, He will give you repentance and forgiveness and grace to overcome, working in you that which is well pleasing in His sight. Your part is to continue to come to Him, to continue to accept the gifts He has to offer.

Thesis 29

God gives us repentance *before* He gives forgiveness.

Let's consider for a few minutes where repentance fits in the sequence of coming to Christ. We noticed earlier that the first step to Christ is a desire for something better. Second, we gain a knowledge of what is better. Third, we are convicted of our sinful condition, and fourth, we realize we are helpless to save ourselves. That's when we give up, or surrender, and come to Christ.

God doesn't expect us to repent before we come to Christ; indeed, it would be impossible for us to do that. We come to Christ first, and then He gives us repentance.

"It was taught by the Jews that before God's love is extended to the sinner, he must first repent. In their view, repentance is a work by which man earns the favor of Heaven. And it was this thought that led the Pharisees to exclaim in astonishment and anger, 'This man receiveth sinners.' According to their ideas He should permit none to approach Him but those who had repented. But in the parable of the lost sheep, Christ teaches that salvation does not come through our seeking after God but through God's seeking after us. 'There is none that understandeth, there is none that seeketh after God. They are all gone out of the way.' Rom. 3:11, 12. We do not repent in order that God may love us, but He reveals to us His love in order that we may repent."—*Christ's Object Lessons,* p. 189.

So after we come to Christ, we come to realize the deadly character of sin by beholding His love for us, and thus become willing to accept His gift of repentance.

Repentance is not something *we* do, even though it's something we do! Repentance is not our work; it is God's work for us. But it does come before forgiveness. And if repentance precedes forgiveness, then repentance also precedes justification. "Whom Christ pardons, He first makes penitent."—*Thoughts From the Mount of Blessing,* p. 7. Acts 2:38 is clear that repentance must take place before forgiveness. "Peter said unto them, Repent and be baptized every one of you in the name of Jesus Christ for the remission of sins."

Sometimes people question the value of becoming so meticulous in trying to isolate and list in order each event in coming to Christ for salvation. It certainly isn't so you can have a list and then check off each item as you proceed and know what to do next! But the enemy of God and man has a steady supply of misunderstandings along the way. And these can bring a barrier between us and God. If we think we are to work on righteousness or faith or surrender or repentance or obedience or any of the other gifts that God is offering to give us freely, we can miss coming to Him. And coming to Him is the only way to receive His gifts.

Many of these separate aspects of coming to Christ—repentance and the new birth and forgiveness and justification—happen almost simultaneously. The purpose of separating them is in order to discuss them, so that we can clearly define what is our work and what is God's work, what is cause and what is result.

The goodness of God leads us to repentance, according to Romans 2:4. We cannot work on repentance, but we can choose to read His word or to listen to the living preacher where the goodness of God is uplifted. We cannot work on repentance, but we can come to Him. We cannot manufacture genuine sorrow for sin; we cannot turn away from sin in our own strength. But we can seek the Lord to do these things for us. God delights to help those who cannot help themselves.

Thesis 30

Worldly sorrow is being sorry we broke a law and got caught. Godly sorrow is being sorry we broke a heart and hurt our best Friend.

Have you ever driven faster than 55 miles per hour? Have you ever been stopped and given a speeding ticket? Were you sorry? For *what* were you sorry? Sorry you got caught? Or sorry you drove too fast?

Have you ever been told to "say you're sorry"? All of us have watched a child who has done something wrong and isn't one bit sorry. Then mother or father comes along and says, "Now say you're sorry."

And the child ducks his head and scuffs his feet and looks thoroughly uncomfortable. Finally he mutters, "Sorry." And the parent lets the matter go. Is the child sorry? Well, he's sorry he had to say he was sorry!

The Bible talks about two kinds of "sorry." "Godly sorrow worketh repentance to salvation not to be repented of: but the sorrow of the world worketh death." 2 Corinthians 7:10. So there's godly sorrow, and there's worldly sorrow. One kind is a matter of relationship; the other is limited to behavior. One kind changes your life; the other kind changes only your actions—and that temporarily. One kind is essential; the other kind isn't worth a dime.

Judas had worldly sorrow. He was sorry he got caught. He waited until the last minute so he could be sure he really had blown it. But when it finally became apparent that Jesus wasn't going to release Himself and that the priests and rulers were going to condemn Him, Judas came forward with his repentance. It says in Matthew 27:3, Judas "repented himself."

It's typical of worldly sorrow that it waits until it is caught red-handed. It's one thing to "repent" after you've been proven guilty, but quite another thing to repent even before you have been accused.

Another Bible example of the wrong kind of sorrow is Cain. He, too, waited until the last minute and then even tried to outtalk God. "Brother? What Brother? Oh, Abel? You mean you expect me to keep up with *him?*"

Godly sorrow, on the other hand, has an entirely different nature. It's being sorry that we hurt someone we love. *The Desire of Ages,* page 300, puts it this way: "We often sorrow because our evil deeds bring unpleasant consequences to ourselves; but this is not repentance. Real sorrow for sin is the result of the working of the Holy Spirit. The Spirit reveals the ingratitude of the heart that has slighted and grieved the Saviour, and brings us in contrition to the foot of the cross. By every sin Jesus is wounded afresh; and as we look upon Him whom we have pierced, we mourn for the sins that have brought anguish upon Him. Such mourning will lead to the renunciation of sin."

This brings us to another compelling reason why repentance has to come as a result of coming to Christ. We cannot sorrow that we have hurt someone we love if we don't love that person! Remember when you were small, and you did some sort of damage to that awful kid next door? And you were supposed to be *sorry?*

As we grow older, we learn (I hope) a little bit about all-encompassing love for mankind, so that our kindness extends beyond the circle of our immediate friends. But it's still true that the more you love someone, the more your heart is broken when you hurt them.

As we learn to know Jesus and to trust the love that He has for us, we will find that we are truly sorry when we bring sorrow to Him. This is the repentance that is godly sorrow, "not to be repented of."

Thesis 31

The only known sin that can't be forgiven is the one for which we don't repent and ask forgiveness.

One day after the church service a little freckled-faced girl, nine or ten years old, pulled my coattail and asked to talk to me. We went to a quiet corner in the sanctuary, and with tears in her eyes and trembling lip, she managed to say, "I think I've committed the unpardonable sin."

Many others have the same concern. There's something frightening about the very phrase "unpardonable sin." It can lead us to picture an angry God, shaking His head and saying, "This time you've gone too far." And struggling Christians from nine to ninety-nine have worried about passing the limits of God's grace and mercy.

The woman taken in adultery was sure she had gone too far. With bowed head and downcast eyes, she silently waited for the stones to fly. She was amazed to discover that the door of mercy was still open for her. She was uncondemned. God still offered His forgiveness and power.

Let's read about the unpardonable sin in Matthew 12:31. Jesus said, "I say unto you, All manner of sin and blasphemy shall be forgiven unto men: but the blasphemy against the Holy Ghost shall not be forgiven unto men."

The first part of the verse is encouraging, *All manner of sin* shall be forgiven. But what does it mean to sin against the Holy Ghost? Simply this: Since it is the work of the Spirit to convict of sin (see John 16:8, 9) and since all manner of sin can be forgiven, then the sin against the Holy Ghost would be to refuse His conviction and refuse to come to repentance.

Forgiveness *is* conditional. If it were not, then everyone in the world would be saved. What are the conditions for forgiveness? First, that we confess our sins. We are told that "if we confess our sins, he is faithful and just to forgive us our sins." 1 John 1:9. Therefore an unpardonable sin would be any sin for which we refuse to confess and seek forgiveness.

Some today have decided that confession is not important. They say that God is a loving Father and that a father would not insist that his children confess their wrong deeds. They say a father forgives his children because he loves them. But that's not what the Bible says. The Bible teaches that confession is important. In order to be forgiven, we must ask for forgiveness and accept it.

How do we accept God's forgiveness? *Steps to Christ,* page 51, says, "If you believe the promise,—believe that you are forgiven and cleansed,—God supplies the fact; you are made whole, just as Christ gave the paralytic power to walk when the man believed that he was healed. It is so if you believe it."

Sometimes we have gotten the idea that the condition for forgiveness is that we never sin again. We promise God, "If you'll just forgive me this one more time—" And then we commit the same sin again and are afraid to come to Him for forgiveness. This is what often causes people to fear they have committed the unpardonable sin.

But the Bible promise is, "Him that cometh to me I will in no wise cast out." John 6:37. There is no expiration date on that as there is on a roll of film. No message that says, "Not good after such-and-such a time." The one who comes to Christ is always, always accepted.

It doesn't matter who you are or what you have done. If you come to Jesus today, ask His forgiveness, accept His gift of repentance and pardon, you will be forgiven. "Jesus loves to have us come to Him just as we are, sinful, helpless, dependent. We may come with all our weakness, our folly, our sinfulness, and fall at His feet in penitence. It is His glory to encircle us in the arms of His love and to bind up our wounds, to cleanse us from all impurity."—*Steps to Christ,* p. 52.

Thesis 32

Forgiveness does the sinner no good unless he accepts it.

You may remember hearing the story a few years ago about the man who was on death row, awaiting his execution. Someone undertook his case, pleading for his life, and he was granted a pardon. But he refused to accept it.

The refusal caused quite a stir in judicial circles. What do you do with a man who refuses to be pardoned? The case finally went to the Supreme Court, and the decision was handed down. If a pardon is given, but the pardon is not accepted, then the pardon cannot be forced upon anyone. And the man who refused to be pardoned went to his death.

Mankind is under sentence of death. We are imprisoned on this planet, awaiting execution. But Jesus has undertaken our case. He came down and died in our place, taking our penalty, becoming our substitute. He offers us pardon. But we can refuse to accept it.

Forgiveness is a two-way transaction. In order for forgiveness to happen, it must be both offered *and* accepted.

Have you ever had it happen on the human level? Has someone wronged you, and have you gone to them and offered forgiveness only to be turned down? Have you ever discovered for yourself that forgiveness has to be two-way? You can be ever so forgiving. You can sincerely be eager for the relationship to be restored. But if the other person doesn't accept the forgiveness you extend, forgiveness doesn't happen.

In Luke 17:3 Jesus told His disciples how they should respond to those who sinned against them. "If thy brother trespass against thee, rebuke him; and if he repent, forgive him." *If he repent,* forgive him. It doesn't say, "If thy brother trespass against thee, forgive him."

In verse 4, Jesus draws the lines even closer. "If he trespass against thee seven times in a day, and seven times in a day turn again to thee, saying, I repent; thou shalt forgive him." Again, the erring one must repent in order to be forgiven.

God has such a high regard for our power of choice that He will not force even His forgiveness upon us. He offers it freely; He encourages us to accept it. But the final choice is ours. We can refuse if we so choose.

As Jesus was being nailed to the cross, He prayed a prayer for those who were crucifying Him. His words were to be repeated through the ages, to this very day, "Father, forgive them; for they know not what they do."

His forgiveness was unlimited, extending even to the very ones who were putting Him to death. He prayed for them specifically. But was His prayer answered? Was it possible for His prayer to be answered? What decided whether His prayer would be answered?

The Desire of Ages, page 745, tells us, "Some by their impenitence would make it an impossibility for the prayer of Christ to be answered for them."

God made provision for forgiveness—abundant and freely offered. Jesus provided the atmosphere for forgiveness. And some accepted, and some refused. For the ones who refused, His forgiveness did no good. It benefited only those who were willing to accept.

Forgiveness is available. The sacrifice of Jesus on the cross sufficed to include in His salvation every soul ever born into this world. The only one who can prevent you from being forgiven is *you.* It is your choice. Forgiveness is yours if you accept it.

Thesis 33

God's forgiveness is not limited, but our acceptance of His forgiveness can be.

He thought he had come up with the perfect crime. For several years now his scheme had appeared to be successful. His government job had turned out to be a steppingstone to financial success. His monthly paycheck was almost a joke, it was so small compared to the amount he regularly embezzled.

Sometimes he worried a little bit. The more he managed to acquire, the more he seemed to spend. But his wife liked nice things, his children were used to the good life, so he pushed aside his fears and kept on with his plan.

Then one day his whole world came crashing in around him. Auditors unexpectedly went over the accounts and he didn't have time to cover his tracks. To his horror and dismay, he was taken into custody, charged with owing the government $10 million. He couldn't imagine where the money had gone. He couldn't imagine what would happen to him now. His wife and children would be humiliated. His beautiful home would be repossessed, and the proceeds from its sale put toward the payment of his debt. But even with all of his assets liquidated, he would still owe millions. And how could he hope to come up with another scheme to recoup his resources if he was sitting in jail?

His day in court finally came. He did the only thing he could do. He went before the judge and pleaded guilty as charged. But he threw himself on the mercy of the court, asking for time to make retribution. To his amazement, the judge suspended his sentence although he had found him guilty.

He walked out of the courtroom a free man. But he was not really free. For he had determined in his own mind that he would somehow repay the money he had embezzled. Otherwise, he felt he would be obligated to the government forever.

On his way home, the first opportunity presented itself. He met a fellow worker who owed him $30. It wasn't much, but it was a start, and besides, he had to live now himself, without the aid of the extra income. So he demanded the $30.

His fellow employee claimed not to have the money. But the debt was long overdue, and he had already been generous enough. So he filed a claim against the man in small claims court.

A few days later, when the case came up, the presiding judge was the same one who had set him free. When the judge saw that the plaintiff was the man who had so recently been in court himself, he was angry. He took the necessary steps at once to reimpose the suspended sentence. And the man was taken to jail, while his charges against his fellow employee were dropped.

This story, recorded in Matthew 18, teaches an important truth about forgiveness. God's forgiveness is unlimited. It is our acceptance of His forgiveness that is sometimes limited and shortcircuits His plan to free us from the condemnation of our sin.

Jesus told this story in answer to Peter's question about how often he should forgive his brother. Jesus gave the famous seventy-times-seven answer, indicating God's unending mercy toward us.

Seventy times seven doesn't mean that God keeps a log, and when we've been forgiven 490 times, that's it. His forgiveness knows no bounds. But we often become discouraged and ashamed, and quit asking. We stop seeking His forgiveness, because *we* think we've gone too far. And thus we place limits on His forgiveness that He never intended.

Or we may find ourselves in sympathy with the man in the story. This man, who was forgiven his debt of $10 million, never really accepted the forgiveness offered. It's true he asked for mercy, but "when the debtor pleaded with his lord for mercy, he had no true sense of the greatness of his debt. He did not realize his helplessness. He hoped to deliver himself."—*Christ's Object Lessons,* p. 245.

His treatment of his fellow worker showed his failure to accept the forgiveness offered. And when the judge reversed the sentence and sent the man to prison, in reality he was merely accepting the man's own choice. For God never forces His forgiveness on anyone.

When we see the true enormity of our sin and our utter helplessness to deliver ourselves, we should not despair. The greater our debt, the greater our need of God's mercy and forgiveness. And because of His great love, there is nothing God wants more than to forgive us and set us free.

FORGIVENESS

Thesis 34

Those who are forgiven much will love much. Those who love much will obey much.

Do you like Peter? It seems his name comes to the top more often than any of the other disciples. Often people confess to identifying with him. He took chances. He dared to ask the wrong questions. He risked giving the wrong answers.

Peter was the one who came to Jesus with the classic question on forgiveness, recorded in Matthew 18:21. "Lord, how oft shall my brother sin against me, and I forgive him? till seven times?" He was mostly asking a rhetorical question; he was pretty sure of his conclusions. Seven times seemed like a lot to Peter. The Pharisees stopped at three. Peter was willing to double their limit, and even go one step farther, arriving at the "perfect" number. Good for Peter!

Now wait a minute before you judge Peter. Of course, you already know Jesus' reply. "I say not unto thee, Until seven times: but, Until seventy times seven." Verse 22. But set that aside for a minute and remember the last time your neighbor or friend or family member did something for which you needed to forgive them. And you forgave them. But they did it again. So you forgave them again. Until seven times. Weren't you about finished forgiving by that time? After all, 490 is a lot of times!

Our family lived for seven years at Pacific Union College in northern California. The college is located up in the mountains, as they say locally, "eight miles from the nearest known sin." It's an Adventist ghetto if you ever saw one. And in that kind of atmosphere, the preacher gets called upon to be a sort of town marshall, judge, and jury all rolled into one.

113

One Sunday the telephone rang. One of the parishioners wanted me to deal with his neighbors. The neighbors' horse had run through his petunias. And he felt that I was the logical one to handle the situation!

The answer I should have given this caller is found in Luke 17:3, 4. "If thy brother trespass against thee, rebuke him; and if he repent, forgive him. And if he trespass against thee seven times in a day, and seven times in a day turn again to thee, saying, I repent; thou shalt forgive him." (Even Peter would probably have thought it was too much if the "seven times" happened in a single day!) What if I had told the man with the petunias, "What you need to do is forgive. And if the neighbor's horse runs through your petunias six more times today, forgive six more times. Biblically speaking, that horse can still come through 489 more times! By which time there will have long since ceased to be any petunias left to run through!"

Jesus recommended unlimited forgiveness. And He would not ask us to be more forgiving than God is, so we know that God's forgiveness is also without limits, as long as we keep coming to Him and asking for pardon and receiving His gift of forgiveness.

But sometimes people get nervous right there. They ask, "Won't that lead to license?" If the neighbors with the horse were forgiven 490 times, or even 7 times in a single day, wouldn't they start thinking their horse had a right to run through the flowers? Won't the teaching of unlimited forgiveness lead us to play fast and loose with God's grace?

Jesus answered that question in His parable to Simon about the two debtors. See Luke 7. He told Simon and Mary and the listening disciples, that whoever is forgiven much, loves much. The more you are forgiven, the more you love.

Now we need to add only one more text, John 14:15. "If you love me, you will obey what I command." NIV.

There you have it. God's forgiveness is limitless. But this does not lead to license, because the one who is forgiven much, loves much. And the more you love, the more you obey. It's just that simple.

"Jesus knows the circumstances of every soul. You may say, I am sinful, very sinful. You may be; but the worse you are, the more you need Jesus. He turns no weeping, contrite one away. He does not tell to any all that He might reveal, but He bids every trembling soul take courage. Freely will He pardon all who come to Him for forgiveness and restoration."—*The Desire of Ages,* p. 568.

Thesis 35

Forgiveness is free, but it is not cheap. It cost the life of God's dear Son.

We were discussing grades one day in a college class I was teaching. I asked the students, "Would you like it better if everyone in the class gets an "A" regardless of how hard he or she works? Or would you rather get an "A" only if you have worked hard for it?"

They said piously, "Oh, we'd rather work hard for our grades."

I didn't believe them! I had heard the usual amount of groans whenever I announced a quiz or test. I had endured the regular supply of excuses for not having work done on time. I had endured the expected number of students who would argue all day to try to get an extra point. I said, "Come on! You're just trying to impress the teacher! Be honest. I'm not grading you on your answer to this! Don't you want a high GPA? Why wouldn't it be good news if every person in this class could have a guaranteed top grade?"

They said, "We wouldn't learn as much. We wouldn't remember as much. We don't appreciate a grade unless we have to work for it."

And I couldn't talk them out of that position!

Do you agree with those students? What makes something more valuable for you—receiving it as a gift, or having to work for it?

If your landlord pays the water bill, does that mean you use water more carefully, or more lavishly? Are you more meticulous about addressing an envelope of company stationery than you are in using your own at home. If you rent a car with unlimited mileage, do you drive the car more or less? When you travel on an expense account, do you stay at the same motel you would choose for your family vacation?

If it's true that human beings tend to place a higher value on things they have had to put forth effort to obtain, then why didn't God set up a system of salvation by works? How can we really appreciate forgiveness or repentance or heaven at last, if it comes only as a gift?

Romans 6:23 says, "The gift of God is eternal life through Jesus Christ our Lord." Acts 5:31 says, "Him hath God exalted with his right hand to be a Prince and a Saviour, for to give repentance to Israel, and forgiveness of sins." So forgiveness and pardon and salvation are gifts, not something we earn or merit. How, then, can we truly value them as we should?

To find an answer to this dilemma, we need to understand the nature of forgiveness. *Thoughts From the Mount of Blessing,* page 114, describes it this way: "God's forgiveness is not merely a judicial act by which He sets us free from condemnation. It is not only forgiveness *for* sin, but reclaiming *from* sin. It is the outflow of redeeming love that transforms the heart."

So forgiveness is not merely a judicial act. It is more than a cleansing of the books of heaven. It is more than a nod of the head toward heaven. It is a restored relationship with a Person. It is a transaction of love.

Love makes a difference, even on a human level in the giving and receiving of gifts. A child can laboriously put together some horrible-looking object made of glue and popsicle sticks, and the parent will value it because of love—in spite of its lack of intrinsic worth. How much more would we value a gift if both the gift and the giver were important to us.

Suppose you were in the hospital with kidney failure, and your brother came forward with the offer of one of his kidneys to save your life. Would you say to him, "Now I want to be able to truly appreciate this kidney, so how about letting me pay you $500 for it?" He would be insulted! The fact that the gift has such a great value and is given by one who loves us so much puts it beyond price.

Love makes a difference. *Need* makes a difference. If you are drowning, and someone throws you a life preserver, do you say, "Now wait a minute. What can I do to pay for this? I can't really appreciate this life preserver unless I've earned it?" No, your sense of need prevents that kind of thinking.

What keeps forgiveness from being cheap, even though it is free? It is recognizing our desperate need. It is understanding how much it cost heaven to be able to offer this kind of gift. It is recognizing the love behind the gift, the deep longing of the Father's heart for reconciliation with His children. With a need like ours—and a love like His—only a gift could answer.

Thesis 36

God forgives sinners, not sins, but the Bible calls this the forgiveness of sins. Jesus died because sins could not be forgiven.

Perhaps I should admit right to begin with that this thesis is playing with words to make a point. Some find this thesis appealing; others find it alarming. But, by means of a story, let's try to understand the truth involved.

One day I was driving the backroads, going well over the speed limit, trying to make up for lost time. I was late for a funeral! But before long, a second cloud of dust joined mine—and inside that second cloud of dust was a state trooper.

He pulled me over to the side of the road, and at first was quite stern in demanding to see my license and my car registration. But after he heard who I was and the nature of my "emergency," he softened up a bit.

He said, "I thought I had a stolen car here. But now I don't know what to do with you. If I give you a ticket, it will be printed in the town newspaper tomorrow, and that will embarrass you before your parishioners. And I don't think a ticket is the answer anyway."

I said, "No sir, I don't think so either!"

Finally he said, "Go on. Go ahead. You're on your own." And he went his way, and I went mine—slowly!

This traffic officer did what God does *not* do, and illustrates the difference I'm trying to draw between the forgiveness of sinners and the forgiveness of sins. The officer "forgave my sin" in exceeding the speed limit. But in so doing, he was not fair to the law of the land which prohibits traveling above a certain speed.

121

God does not change His law. He does not make exceptions. When man transgresses, it is not one of His options to simply say, "That's OK. Never mind. We'll overlook it this time."

"Had it been possible for the law to be changed or abrogated, then Christ need not have died. But to abrogate the law would be to immortalize transgression, and place the world under Satan's control. It was because the law was changeless, because man could be saved only through obedience to its precepts, that Jesus was lifted up on the cross."—*The Desire of Ages,* pp. 762, 763.

What God does is to forgive *sinners.* There is a difference! If the traffic officer had treated me as God treats me, he would have had no option but to give me a ticket. I would have been called into court, and the judge would have declared me guilty and fined me a certain amount of money.

If I didn't have the money required, I would have to spend time in jail. And when that was determined, the police officer would have stepped forward, taken out his wallet, and paid the fine himself so that I could go free. If he had done that, he would have upheld the law and at the same time saved me from the penalty of my lawbreaking.

Mankind broke the law of God. Because God could not forgive sins, He could not shake His head at Adam and Eve and say, "Go ahead. You're on your own." If He had done that, His whole universe would have been in jeopardy.

The government of our country sometimes lets us get by with quite a bit. We can sometimes break the law and not get caught. In fact, some estimate that at least 80 percent of crimes go unresolved. Even when we are caught, we may be permitted to escape the penalty of our sins.

But not so in the divine government. Sin does not go undetected, and it cannot be passed over. Romans 6:23 is always true: "The wages of sin is death."

Because of His love, God found a way out. The death of Christ on the cross freed Him to forgive *sinners.* Thus He secures both His justice and our deliverance.

Thesis 37

Christ died for our sins according to the Scripture.

You be the judge. It is the middle of World War II. Hitler is captured and brought into your courtroom. The evidence against him comes in, horror upon horror. You hear about the gas chambers. You hear about people forced to dig their own graves and then gunned down into them. You hear about starving children dragged screaming from their parents, only to watch them mutilated by German soldiers. You see photographs of open sores, bloated corpses, vacant eyes. You are the judge. What sentence are you going to pronounce?

Wait a minute now! Be sure you do the loving thing! Do you want to gain a reputation as a harsh, angry judge? If you decide that Hitler needs to be punished, won't that drag you down to his level?

A concept talked about quite a lot in recent times—is that God is a God of love and therefore wouldn't hurt anybody. It denounces as pagan the thought that Christ's death was necessary. It says, "God is not an angry God, needing to be appeased. He is not a God of judgment. What appears to be divine judgment is simply the result of our own poor choices. It wouldn't be the loving thing for God to bring destruction and death."

Perhaps Hitler is an extreme example. Let's try one from the Old Testament. The children of Israel have been having a party. They've taken advantage of the fact that Moses was out of town and Aaron was in charge. With his help, they've constructed a golden calf, and just at the height of the celebration, Moses returns unexpectedly. Do you remember the result? The ones who repented were forced to drink their idol, and the ones who didn't repent were killed. Sounds pretty harsh. Did God do the loving thing in that situation?

"It was the mercy of God that thousands should suffer, to prevent the necessity of visiting judgments upon millions. In order to save the many, He must punish the few. Furthermore, as the people had cast off their allegiance to God, they had forfeited the divine protection, and, deprived of their defense, the whole nation was exposed to the power of their enemies. Had not the evil been promptly put away, they would soon have fallen a prey to their numerous and powerful foes. It was necessary for the good of Israel, and also as a lesson to all succeeding generations, that crime should be promptly punished. And it was no less a mercy to the sinners themselves that they should be cut short in their evil course. Had their life been spared, the same spirit that led them to rebel against God would have been manifested in hatred and strife among themselves, and they would eventually have destroyed one another. It was in love to the world, in love to Israel, and even to the transgressors, that crime was punished with swift and terrible severity."—*Patriarchs and Prophets,* pp. 325, 326.

Sin is never for free. Sin brings death, and it is not possible to simply cancel the consequences. In one way only can justice deal with the reality of sin, and that is if another takes the penalty. "Christ died for our sins according to the scripture." 1 Corinthians 15:3. That is the simple statement of the Bible truth on the subject. Isaiah 53:5 says, "He was wounded for our transgressions, he was bruised for our iniquities."

Justice is just as loving as is mercy. If your boy is beating on your girl, you don't love either your boy or your girl unless you do something to stop it. The death of Christ in behalf of those who will accept His sacrifice, and the ultimate punishment of the ones who do not accept in the lake of fire, is the most loving thing the Judge of the universe can do in the face of the awfulness of sin. The death of Christ and the final punishment of the wicked reveals His love as much as does His mercy extended to the repenting sinner. True love must find justice and mercy combined.

Thesis 38

The cross made it possible for God to be just and yet to forgive anyone.

At first he was exhilarated. True, he had lost the latest battle and had been cast out of heaven, but now Lucifer had his own kingdom with more than one third of the heavenly angels under his direct control. Surely with this kind of a beginning he would soon be able to regroup and make another attack—and the next battle might end in his favor.

But before long the problems in his government began to manifest themselves. There was no unity in the ranks. Now that direct conflict with the Son of God had ended, the fallen angels began scrapping among themselves. Their constant bickering was a source of discomfort even for Satan!

But an even deeper conflict was going on in his heart. Satan was lonely. He felt it most keenly at the hour when the heavenly choirs would be leading out in praising God. He used to be the leader of those choirs. And the awfulness of the choice he had made began to make itself felt. He looked ahead to a future that was blacker than anything he could ever have imagined.

The book *The Story of Redemption* gives this description: "Satan trembled as he viewed his work. He was alone in meditation upon the past, the present, and his future plans. His mighty frame shook as with a tempest. An angel from heaven was passing. He called him and entreated an interview with Christ. This was granted him. He then related to the Son of God that he repented of his rebellion and wished again the favor of God. . . . Christ wept at Satan's woe but told him, as the mind of God, that he could never be received into heaven. Heaven must not be placed in jeopardy. All heaven would be marred should he be received back, for sin and rebellion originated with him. The seeds of rebellion were still within him."—Page 26.

Satan went forth from this interview with Christ with the determination to try another ploy. He determined to bring about the fall of mankind. This would accomplish what he had failed to accomplish by other methods. Satan's first charges against God had questioned His justice. Now he would have a test case to prove his point.

If mankind sinned, this would prove that the law of God was unjust and could not be obeyed. At the very least, Satan could then take over the rulership of Earth. But if God should offer some plan to restore mankind to Heaven's favor, then Satan would have the opportunity he was really after—a chance to be reinstated himself. For if God could allow mankind another chance, it would be only fair for Satan to receive another opportunity as well.

But the mind of God already held provision for just such an emergency. From eternity a plan had existed to accomplish both the recovery of fallen mankind and the vindication of God from Satan's charges.

Through the death of Christ on the cross, God "might be just, and the justifier of him which believeth in Jesus." Romans 3:26. The sacrifice of Christ in our behalf enabled God to maintain both justice and forgiveness. The cross revealed God's justice, while at the same time it provided a method by which man could be forgiven without destroying God's justice.

For Satan, who had sinned deliberately in the full light and knowledge of the love of God, no greater manifestation of that love was possible to change his rebellious heart. But to mankind, deceived and confused, God could offer another chance. For those who were willing to accept it, the love and justice and mercy of God revealed in the death of Christ would make a difference. For those who are willing to accept it, a way of salvation has been provided.

Thesis 39

The death of Christ was necessary in order for us to be forgiven.

Suppose you were to decide that you wanted to reveal God's love to the people of Chicago. So you move to downtown Chicago and begin walking the streets, helping those who are in trouble, taking time to listen to those who are lonely, and doing all you can to share God's love with those you meet.

But Chicago is a dangerous place, particularly after dark. And in walking the streets after midnight, you are inevitably taking a risk. You get by with your plan for a time and are able to be a blessing to a number of people. But one night you pass a dark alley where some desperate criminal waits, and you lose your life.

Those who were acquainted with you there in Chicago find out what happened to you. They tell others how you died to show God's love. And so your death becomes meaningful because of the chances you were willing to take to reach the people of Chicago with the love of God.

Do you think this is a good analogy for Christ's death on the cross? Was His death necessary in order for us to be forgiven? Or was the death of Christ incidental? Did He come to this earth solely to reveal the love of God, but die simply because earth is a dangerous place to be? Or was His death an integral part of the plan to save mankind?

There is a "moral influence theory" of the atonement which insists that Christ's death was not essential. It insists that mankind could have been forgiven apart from His death. One of the errors this theory is trying to counteract is the idea of an angry God needing a "pound of flesh" in order to appease His wrath. And it's true that the purpose of Christ's death was not to satisfy God's vengeance. God was in Christ, reconciling the world unto Himself. But was the death of Christ necessary for other reasons?

There is this insight in the book *The Great Controversy,* page 73: "Jesus died as a sacrifice for man because the fallen race can do nothing to recommend themselves to God. The merits of a crucified and risen Saviour are the foundation of the Christian's faith."

The priests and rulers gathered about the cross on the day of the crucifixion. They were unwilling to accept a crucified Christ. They said, "If he be the King of Israel, let him now come down from the cross, and we will believe him." Matthew 27:42. Is it possible to echo that same thought today? Is it possible to want Christ down from the cross, in order to be able to believe?

It is a blow to human pride to admit that we need to be saved, rather than educated. But the whole basis of the Christian faith is the premise that mankind needs a Saviour.

The Bible teaches repeatedly that Christ is our Substitute. Perhaps the best-known passage is in Isaiah 53. "Surely he hath borne our griefs, and carried our sorrows: yet we did esteem him stricken, smitten of God, and afflicted. But he was wounded for our transgressions, he was bruised for our iniquities: the chastisement of our peace was upon him; and with his stripes we are healed. All we like sheep have gone astray; we have turned every one to his own way; and the Lord hath laid on him the iniquity of us all." Verses 4-6.

The entire sacrificial system, from Adam and Eve at the gates of Eden to the temple ritual of Jesus' day, was based on the understanding that a substitute was to come to take the place of sinful man in order that he might be saved. Christ was "the lamb slain from the foundation of the world." Revelation 13:8.

However crucifying it may be to the human heart, salvation comes only in accepting the crucified and risen Saviour. "Kneeling in faith at the cross, he has reached the highest place to which man can attain."—*The Acts of the Apostles,* p. 210.

Thesis 40

We can add nothing to what Jesus did at the cross, but God can add plenty.

At the General Conference session in Dallas, Texas, one of the items on the agenda was a discussion and reexamination of church doctrines. One of the beliefs that the church gave particular attention to was the doctrine of the atonement. Comments, pro and con, flew back and forth—some insisting that we believe in a complete atonement, others sure that we believe in an incomplete atonement. I was sitting in the balcony, watching H. M. S. Richards, Sr., sitting down below on the main floor, reading his Bible, apparently oblivious to his surroundings!

One time he commented on a particular Bible Conference he had attended, "I received such a blessing that week—I was able to read through the entire New Testament while at those meetings!" But I was just wishing he would get up and say something to help us all out when W. G. C. Murdoch went to the platform. He said, "Seventh-day Adventists have always believed in a complete atonement that is not yet completed."

Christ's sacrifice on the cross was a complete sacrifice. When Jesus cried, "It is finished," He was telling the truth. He had finished the work He had come to this earth to accomplish. "The battle had been won. His right hand and His holy arm had gotten Him the victory. As a Conqueror He planted His banner on the eternal heights. Was there not joy among the angels? All heaven triumphed in the Saviour's victory. Satan was defeated, and knew that his kingdom was lost."—*The Desire of Ages,* p. 758.

9—95 T

And there is nothing we can add to His sacrifice. Our good works add nothing. Our obedience or self-sacrifice add nothing. We can only accept the complete sacrifice of Christ in our behalf.

But the atonement was not yet completed. In the Old Testament analogy of the Day of Atonement, the day did not end when the high priest offered the sacrifice. The sins of the people had yet to be transferred to the scapegoat, and the scapegoat had to be sent away into the wilderness. When Jesus died on the cross, the battle to become our Substitute for sin had been won. But the war wasn't (and isn't) over yet.

If God intended to do nothing more toward our recovery after the cross, then we should never have known a day of pain or suffering or sorrow or death ever since. When Christ came forth on the morning of the resurrection, everybody who had ever lived and died should have come up with Him—not just the few "firstfruits." When He ascended to heaven, all of those who had accepted Him from Adam to the thief on the cross should have gone up to heaven with Him. But that didn't happen, as we well know.

It would be a gross misunderstanding to think that anything we can do can add anything to what Jesus did for us at the cross. It would be an equal misunderstanding to think that the entire plan of salvation was completed at the cross. The cross is the foundation of the Christian faith—but no building is completed when the foundation is completed, no matter how solid and firm that foundation may be.

The additional time necessary for Satan's purposes to become fully known and recognized by the entire universe is also a part of God's plan. The giving of the gospel to all the world, that each individual might have an adequate opportunity to accept or reject Him, is a part of God's plan. The coming of Jesus in power and glory to take His children to their heavenly home is a part of God's plan. The thousand years in heaven, giving each person the chance to examine the records of the judgment and know that God has been fair and just, is a part of God's plan. The final confrontation with the armies of the enemy, the unveiling of Satan before the watching throng when every knee shall bow and every tongue shall confess that Jesus Christ is Lord—that's a part of God's plan too.

And the destruction of the wicked, root and branch, followed by the re-creation of the earth, these too are part of God's wonderful plan for our salvation and restoration. He had only just begun. The end will be more glorious than we can imagine, for "since the beginning of the world men have not heard, nor perceived by the ear, neither hath the eye seen, O God, beside thee, what he hath prepared for him that waiteth for him." Isaiah 64:4.

Thesis 41

Staying with Jesus is just as important as coming to Him.

Which is more important, getting married, or staying married? I've had fun asking this question of various audiences around the country and having them raise their hands to indicate their answer. But after we consider it for a few minutes, the question that always gets the largest show of hands is when I finally ask, "How many think it's a stupid question?"

Obviously, getting married doesn't mean much if you don't plan to stay married. And you can't stay married if you've never gotten married in the first place.

But how often do we remember that principle in the Christian life? Coming to Jesus is important, no doubt about it. But that is only the beginning. In order to remain a Christian, we must continue to come to Him. It is just as important to stay with Jesus as it is to come to Him in the first place.

"However complete may have been our consecration at conversion, it will avail us nothing unless it be renewed daily."—Ellen G. White, *Review and Herald,* January 6, 1885. "To follow Jesus requires wholehearted conversion at the start, and a repetition of this conversion every day."—Ellen G. White Comments, *S.D.A. Bible Commentary,* vol. 1, p. 1113. Jesus said, "If any man will come after me, let him deny himself, and take up his cross daily, and follow me." Luke 9:23.

Christianity is more than a one-time decision—it is a way of life. And while this seems to be an elementary truth, many have missed it and discovered to their dismay that it's then uphill business to serve the Lord.

We understand how daily commitment is necessary in a marriage. We know it's true in the work-a-day world. It doesn't matter how brilliantly you shine at the job interview, or how hard you work the first day on the new job, if you stop right there, you will soon find yourself unemployed. You can start an exercise program and work yourself breathless the first time around, but unless you keep at it day after day, you won't see any results. Giving birth to a baby is a complicated procedure, but your job as a parent is just beginning when your child is born. A lot more is involved in getting an education than showing up for registration day, important as that is.

If it is so readily apparent in the things of here and now that a one-time decision is insufficient, then how much more should we recognize the importance of commitment when the things of eternity are involved.

Sometimes I have talked about the method for staying with Jesus and the importance of spending time with Him day by day. Then someone will come along after the service and say, "I tried that, and it didn't work."

"How long did you try?"

"Three days."

Shouldn't we be willing at least to give God equal time with the things of this life? There may be some job that you simply can't perform. There may be some marriage situations that are impossible. There may be some types of education for which you are not qualified. But when it comes to the Christian life, only one thing is required: that you come to Jesus, and that you keep coming to Him day by day. If you will keep coming to Him, God has made Himself responsible for taking care of everything else that needs to happen in your life. *The Desire of Ages,* page 302: "If the eye is kept fixed on Christ, the work of the Spirit ceases not until the soul is conformed to His image."

Thesis 42

Assurance of salvation continues through the daily personal relationship with Jesus.

"And this is the record, that God hath given to us eternal life, and this life is in his Son. He that hath the Son hath life; and he that hath not the Son of God hath not life." 1 John 5:11, 12.

Do you have the Son? Do you know what it means to have the Son? The apostle John indicates here that having the Son, or not having the Son, is the factor that determines whether we have life eternal. But what does "having the Son" mean?

Sometimes the words and phrases we use in describing and defining the Christian life are confusing. When I was a teenager, I found it very frustrating to constantly hear all of the catch phrases of Christianity without knowing what they meant.

What does it mean to "have the Son"? What does it mean to "fall on the Rock"? How do you "behold the Lamb"? How do you "reach out your hand and take His"? We use a lot of these kinds of expressions, don't we? The Bible uses them. The inspired writings to our church use them.

Early in my ministry I was so frustrated with trying to act like a Christian and talk like a Christian and preach like a Christian, when in fact I *wasn't* a Christian, that I was just about ready to give up the whole business. But one day I decided to make one more attempt. I took the book *Steps to Christ* and read through it, underlining everything it told me to do. And when I finished, I had underlined practically the whole book. Not only that, but much of what I had underlined was these intangible phrases.

I was on my way to throw the book in the fire, when something stopped me. Because even though I was farther than ever from the answers I had been looking for, something had happened inside that I could not explain, but could not deny.

So I decided to do one thing more: I would go back through the book and underline twice everything it told me to do that I already knew how to do.

And that was how I began to understand the basics in living the Christian life. I underlined three things—read your Bible, pray, and tell someone else what you got out of the first two.

Whenever you come across an intangible phrase, either in the Bible or in what we call the spirit of prophecy, if you look a little closer, you'll discover that it's talking about one of these three tangibles that make all of the intangibles tangible!

With that in mind, let's look again at 1 John 5:11, 12. "He that hath the Son hath life." Why, we use those same words in our everyday language!

We say, "I have a friend." "I have a wife." "She has a husband." What are we talking about? We're describing a relationship with that person.

If we have the Son, we have a relationship with the Son of God. We are talking about spending time in communication with Him. We speak to Him in prayer. We listen to Him speak to us in His Word. We work with Him in service and outreach to others.

So if the basis of eternal life is to "have the Son," then the basis of eternal life is to have a relationship with Jesus, to know what it means to spend time in fellowship and communion with Him day by day.

Our assurance of salvation is not based on church membership. It is not based on doctrinal purity. It is not based on behavior. It is based on an ongoing relationship with a Person.

"Those who will keep the eye fixed upon the life of the Lord Jesus will gain an abundant entrance into His spiritual temple."—Ellen G. White Comments, *S.D.A. Bible Commentary*, vol. 6, p. 1086. "No renewed heart can be kept in a condition of sweetness without the daily application of the salt of the word. Divine grace must be received daily, or no man will stay converted."—Ellen G. White, *Review and Herald,* September 14, 1897.

As you come to Jesus day by day, accepting anew of His grace and seeking to know Him better and trust Him more, you can have the assurance of eternal life.

Thesis 43

Christians should know that they have the assurance of salvation today.

What do you answer if someone asks you, "Are you saved?" Have you ever had it happen? How did you respond?

The inspired writings to our church give us some pretty strong warnings against saying, "I am saved." Let's notice a couple of them here.

"We are never to rest in a satisfied condition, and cease to make advancement, saying, 'I am saved.' When this idea is entertained, the motives for watchfulness, for prayer, for earnest endeavor to press onward to higher attainments, cease to exist. No sanctified tongue will be found uttering these words till Christ shall come, and we enter in through the gates into the city of God. Then, with the utmost propriety, we may give glory to God and to the Lamb for eternal deliverance. As long as man is full of weakness—for of himself he cannot save his soul—he should never dare to say, 'I am saved.' "—*Selected Messages,* bk. 1, p. 314.

A similar paragraph, found in *Christ's Object Lessons,* page 155, reads: "Never can we safely put confidence in self or feel, this side of heaven, that we are secure against temptation. Those who accept the Saviour, however sincere their conversion, should never be taught to say or to feel that they are saved. This is misleading. Every one should be taught to cherish hope and faith; but even when we give ourselves to Christ and know that He accepts us, we are not beyond the reach of temptation. God's word declares, 'Many shall be purified, and made white, and tried.' Daniel 12:10. Only he who endures the trial will receive the crown of life."

Notice that these warnings are against the idea of once saved, always saved. They are speaking about thinking that just because we have once *been* saved that it is automatic that we will ultimately *be* saved. There can be a real difference between saying, "I am saved today," and saying, "I will be saved in heaven."

One person came up with a pretty good answer to cover both bases: when asked, "Are you saved?" he responded, "So far!"

But let's limit our attention for the moment to the question of *today*. Are you saved today? How do you answer? Do you say, "I hope so," or "I think so," or, "I guess I'll find out when the judgment day arrives"? Or can you comfortably answer, "Yes, I have the assurance of salvation today"?

The question of personal salvation is the most-oft-asked question in Christian circles. Whenever surveys give Christians the opportunity to list their most urgent question, this one always rises to the top. It is the common question for young and old alike. If you ask an audience to write down the one question they would like to ask, if they could know for sure they'd get the right answer, questions about assurance of salvation are always in the majority. "Will I be in heaven?" "Will I be saved?" "Will I make it?" It's sort of a self-centered concern! In fact, it is one of the major methods the devil uses to focus our attention on ourselves and to cause us to lose sight of Jesus. *Steps to Christ,* page 72, warns us about it. It says, "We should not make self the center and indulge anxiety and fear as to whether we shall be saved. All this turns the soul away from the Source of our strength. Commit the keeping of your soul to God, and trust in Him. Talk and think of Jesus. Let self be lost in Him. Put away all doubt; dismiss your fears."

We must always live the Christian life one day at a time. Seek God for fellowship and communion one day at a time. Come to Him for repentance and forgiveness one day at a time. Lay all our plans at His feet, to be carried out or given up as His providence shall indicate, one day at a time. Come to Him for the outpouring of His Spirit, strength for trial, wisdom for service, one day at a time. And as we do this, we can accept His assurance of salvation one day at a time. "If you are right with God today, you are ready if Christ should come today."—*In Heavenly Places,* p. 227.

If you have been trying to base your assurance of salvation on your past experience with God—even if the past experience happened as recently as yesterday—then you are making a mistake. If you have been trying to somehow gather up enough assurance to last you through to the end of your life—even if your life should end tomorrow—then you're in trouble. But you can have the assurance of salvation today. And if you take the time day by day to make sure of your acceptance of God's acceptance, the end of your life on this earth will find you among the saved for eternity.

Thesis 44

The Bible teaches once-saved always-saved as long as you keep saved.

I went one night to hear a Nazarene preacher who said, "We believe in once saved, always saved, as long as you keep saved." That's one belief Seventh-day Adventists have in common with the Nazarene church!

A large cross section of the evangelical Christian world believes that all that is necessary in order to be saved is to nod your head toward heaven once during your lifetime, and your eternal salvation is assured. They believe that regardless of what choices you make, or the direction of your life after the point of the initial decision for Christ, that in the end you will find yourself ushered in through the pearly gates to the city of God.

But the Bible teaching on this subject is very clear. "Because iniquity shall abound, the love of many shall wax cold. But he that shall endure unto the end, the same shall be saved." Matthew 24:12, 13.

Jesus taught the same principle in John 15. He was speaking His last words to the disciples on their way to Gethsemane. He pointed to the vineyards, visible in the moonlit night, and tried once again to explain about the relationship they must sustain to Him in order to have life. He said in verse 6, "If a man abide not in me, he is cast forth as a branch, and is withered; and men gather them, and cast them into the fire, and they are burned." So it is possible to be a branch, but not to abide, or stay with the Vine. And when that separation continues, the time comes that the branch is removed.

In His parable about the wedding feast in Matthew 22 Jesus also spoke of the possibility of making a beginning, but not keeping on in the Christian life. The king had prepared the feast. The man had accepted the invitation to the feast. He had made a start. But he had neglected or refused to put on the wedding garment, and when the king came in to examine the guests, the man was found lacking. The king gave the command, "Bind him hand and foot, and take him away, and cast him into outer darkness; there shall be weeping and gnashing of teeth." Verse 13.

"Sinful man can find hope and righteousness only in God, and no human being is righteous any longer than he has faith in God and maintains a vital connection with Him."—*Testimonies to Ministers,* p. 367.

As we have already noticed, the assurance of salvation continues as long as our relationship with God continues, as long as we continue to accept His gifts of repentance and forgiveness and grace. Continuing salvation is based upon this faith relationship with Him, not upon our behavior or our performance. And no relationship continues any longer than the relationship continues.

We know from our human relationships that it is possible to have had a relationship with someone at one time, but to no longer have that relationship today. Unless a relationship is kept alive by continuing fellowship and communication and contact, it will inevitably die.

The same is true in our relationship with God. The Bible faithfully records the examples of those such as Enoch, Moses, Daniel, and Paul, who continued to walk with God to the end of their lives. Paul was able to say near the close of his life, "I have fought a good fight, I have finished my course, I have kept the faith: henceforth there is laid up for me a crown of righteousness." 2 Timothy 4:7, 8. He did *not* say, "I joined the right side; I started the right course; I once had faith." No, he had *kept* the faith, enduring until the end.

And the Bible also tells us about those who began with God, but who fell by the wayside and lost the salvation they once had. Cain began by offering morning and evening sacrifices with the rest of the family. But he did not endure until the end. King Saul started out converted, a humble child of God. But he took over control of his own life and ended his own life as a result. Balaam was at one time a prophet of God, but in spite of his talking donkey, the angel who appeared to warn him, and the voice of God in dreams of the night to advise him, he was more interested in his own glory than in God's glory and became an ally to the enemies of the people of God. Judas was one of the inner circle; he listened to the words and saw the works of Christ. He received a place as a missionary and joined with the other disciples in healing the sick and casting out devils and raising the dead. But he walked away from it all and betrayed his Lord.

To be saved once is important. To continue to accept salvation is equally important.

Thesis 45

Peace does not come from victory, but victory comes from peace.

She had been heavily involved in the counterculture, including drugs and all the rest of it. Now she was trying to find her way back and had discovered it wasn't easy. She had become friends with one of the young men on campus, and he brought her to my office for counsel.

As she described her dilemma, telling of her disillusionment with what the world had to offer, but admitting to her inability to change the habit patterns to which she had become enslaved, something clicked in my mind. She sounded like a description given in the book *Steps to Christ,* page 49.

So we opened the book and read it together.

"As your conscience has been quickened by the Holy Spirit, you have seen something of the evil of sin, of its power, its guilt, its woe; and you look upon it with abhorrence. You feel that sin has separated you from God, that you are in bondage to the power of evil. The more you struggle to escape, the more you realize your helplessness. Your motives are impure; your heart is unclean. You see that your life has been filled with selfishness and sin. You long to be forgiven, to be cleansed, to be set free. Harmony with God, likeness to Him—what can you do to obtain it?"

"Yes," she said. "That's me. That's my problem. Quick! Tell me the answer. What can I do?"

Stop with me for a moment and consider what the answer might be. The first paragraph describes a messed-up life. The Holy Spirit has been working on the heart, and the person has become aware of a great need. But he has also become aware of a great helplessness. He can't seem to gain the victory over his life of sin, and he is asking how to be free. What does he need in order to be forgiven and cleansed?

If you are a behaviorist, your first response would be in the area of performance. You might say, "This person needs to try harder to do what's right. He mustn't give up. He must choose to obey God, and God will then give him whatever power he needs to follow through on that choice."

If you are a relationist, your first response might be that the person described here needs to read the Bible and pray more.

If you are a religionist, you might advise that the solution lies in joining a church, associating with other believers.

But what is the answer given in *Steps to Christ?* The very next sentence, still on page 49, says: "It is *peace* that you need." (Emphasis supplied.)

What an answer! That sounds like telling a man who is dying of thirst that he needs water. Or telling a child dying of starvation that he needs food. Or telling a family on the verge of bankruptcy that it needs money. How can someone have peace when his life is in confusion?

But wait. "It is peace that you need—Heaven's forgiveness and peace and love in the soul. Money cannot buy it, intellect cannot procure it, wisdom cannot attain to it; you can never hope, by your own efforts, to secure it. But God offers it to you as a gift, 'without money and without price.'. . . It is yours if you will but reach out your hand and grasp it."—*Ibid.*

Consider a child who is growing and developing. Does he ever make mistakes? Does he ever fall or fail? Does he ever do foolish things? How should we treat him? It is a universal and timeless principle that the only one who can grow out of his mistakes and failures is the one who is loved and accepted while he is making them.

What about learning to drive? Do you remember what that was like? Did you do it all right the first time around? The only one who is going to learn to drive is the one who is allowed to make mistakes and still keep trying.

Have you ever started a new job? Did you do everything perfectly from the first day onward? Or did your boss expect you to take some time to learn? When a new employee comes to work, even the business world makes allowances for his inexperience. He isn't fired the first time he fails at something. Instead, he is accepted and affirmed while he learns. That's the only environment in which a person can relax and remember the right way to do things.

Jesus said to the woman taken in adultery, "Neither do I condemn thee: go, and sin no more." John 8:11. The only person who can hope to go and sin no more is the one who knows he's not condemned. Peace must come first. Peace brings release.

Thesis 46

One reason we keep sinning is that we don't believe we are forgiven. Assurance leads to victory. Uncertainty leads to defeat.

In a church I pastored several years ago, one family adopted a little five-year-old girl. Born to a "junkie" mother, the child had already experienced more of the ugly side of life than most people do in a lifetime. She had learned to survive, but she didn't know how to live. She knew how to hate, but not how to love. In many ways she seemed an impossible case.

A series of foster homes lay behind her. She would speak in passing of "Mother Karen," and "Mama Becky," and "Mommy Ann." All of them had let her down. Now she had been adopted by a Christian family and promised a permanent home. But she didn't know about permanence. All she understood was temporary—and she was not about to let herself be hurt again.

She was so sure that she was going to be abandoned, that she did everything she could to hurry up the process. She was a master at disrupting a household. Because she had been abused beyond belief from babyhood, no punishment could control her. At times her new family despaired of ever reaching her.

As long as she remained convinced that her bad behavior was going to result in her rejection, she continued to rebel. The breakthrough came for her only when she finally understood that no matter how bad she was, she was still going to be accepted. Only when her new family finally communicated unconditional acceptance to her was she able to begin to heal.

151

Only then did she discover that disobedience was no longer necessary.

One of the things that helped was for her to clearly understand the consequences of certain actions. The consequences were fair, not harsh. But she was not allowed to misbehave "for free." At the same time, she slowly came to understand that the consequence of disobeying was *not* to be rejected and sent away. For as long as she was willing to remain in the household, her place was secure.

Sometimes we have looked at God in the same way this child looked at her new parents. We have been so sure that He was going to reject us because of what we are, that we keep on being what we are! We keep on sinning because we don't believe we are forgiven. We remain defeated because we have no assurance that He accepts us even while we grow.

Does this mean that sin is OK, that we can break His law and go unpunished? No, wrongdoing does have consequences. But being rejected by God doesn't happen to be one of them—as long as we remain "in the family" and continue to come to Him for healing and forgiveness and power.

Steps to Christ, page 52, puts it this way: "Some seem to feel that they must be on probation, and must prove to the Lord that they are reformed, before they can claim His blessing. But they may claim the blessing of God even now. They must have His grace, the Spirit of Christ, to help their infirmities, or they cannot resist evil. Jesus loves to have us come to Him just as we are, sinful, helpless, dependent. We may come with all our weakness, our folly, our sinfulness, and fall at His feet in penitence. It is His glory to encircle us in the arms of His love, and to bind up our wounds, to cleanse us from all impurity."

First John 3:2 says, "Beloved, now are we the sons of God, and it doth not yet appear what we shall be: but we know that, when he shall appear, we shall be like him; for we shall see him as he is."

Our part is to make sure that *now* we continue in relationship with Him as His sons and daughters. His part is to insure that whatever needs to be done to make us like Him, will be done in time.

Jesus loves to have us come to Him just as we are, for that is the only way we *can* come. He sets no limits on the number of times we can come and still be accepted. He loves us because we are His children, not because of any good in us. And when we finally come to understand that we are loved and accepted by Him, we will begin to heal. Accepting His acceptance makes the difference.

Thesis 47

Righteousness by faith is an experience, not just a theory.

Let me give you a recipe for strawberry shortcake, You put a piece of cake in the bottom of a large bowl. Some people use spongecake. Some people prefer a sort of biscuitlike substance. Some people use a plain white cake. But whichever you use, you then pile on top of it a mound of strawberries. If it's winter, you may have to use frozen strawberries. But fresh ones are the best. And then on top of the strawberries, you put lots of whipped cream.

The details and methods may vary slightly from person to person. But one thing is certain. Strawberry shortcake is an experience, not just a theory! All of the variations of the three ingredients—cake, strawberries, and whipped topping—have only one goal in the end. In order to appreciate strawberry shortcake fully, you have to experience it.

We've talked about the three tangible ingredients in the Christian life that go to make up this thing called "relationship." We've talked about Bible study, prayer, and Christian witness or service or outreach. In this section I'm going to deal with the "recipe" for a meaningful devotional life.

But over and above it all, you must clearly understand one fact: The theory apart from the experience is of little value. In order to benefit from the "recipe," you must taste it for yourself!

There is a vast difference between knowing someone and simply knowing *about* someone. You can read about Abraham Lincoln or Florence Nightingale. You can know their history, memorize their sayings, admire their lives. But you cannot have a personal relationship with them. You cannot know *them*; you can only know *about* them.

Many Christians have been content to know about God. They gather information from His Word on occasion. They discuss Him in Sabbath School class week by week. They realize that He is loving and just and merciful. They admire Him from afar. But they never come to know Him for themselves in a personal one-to-one communion.

The psalmist says, "O taste and see that the Lord is good: blessed is the man that trusteth in him." Psalm 34:8. *The Desire of Ages*, page 347, tells us: "To talk of religion in a casual way, to pray without soul hunger and living faith, avails nothing. A nominal faith in Christ, which accepts Him merely as the Saviour of the world, can never bring healing to the soul. The faith that is unto salvation is not a mere intellectual assent to the truth. . . . It is not enough to believe *about* Christ; we must believe *in* Him. The only faith that will benefit us is that which embraces Him as a personal Saviour; which appropriates His merits to ourselves."

The recipe is important. But the tasting and experiencing is even more important. You can read about a good recipe, but only you can make the decision to try it out for yourself.

Is there a recipe for relationship with Christ? Here's one that many of us have found meaningful. Take time, alone, at the beginning of every day, to seek Jesus through His Word and through prayer.

Take time. Relationships don't happen in an instant. We hear a lot these days about "quality" time versus "quantity" time. But there are limits to how much quality you can receive or give if the quantity is marginal.

Alone: One-to-one is where the deepest communication happens. It's true in marriages, in families, in friendships. It's also true with God.

At the beginning. We are invited to give God top priority, to begin our day with Him—not save Him for the last minute before going to bed.

Of every day: Regularity is important. Whether you're talking about an exercise program, learning to play the piano, or making a friend, random contact is not enough.

To seek Jesus. The focus of the devotional life will always be Him. The devotional life is not intended to be a study of prophecy or doctrine or temperance. It is getting acquainted with a Person.

Through His Word and through prayer. He speaks to us through His Word; we respond to Him through prayer. Talking and listening are the basic elements of communication.

Don't stop with just a recipe, whether it's for strawberry shortcake or how to know God. Experience it for yourself. Only then will you truly understand its worth.

Thesis 48

The Christian's devotional life is not optional. The relationship with God is the entire basis of the ongoing Christian life.

Alan never intended to oversleep. He had set his alarm for 6:30 a.m. as usual, but he had been up late the night before. And when the alarm went off, he awakened only enough to push the "off" button and then went back to sleep. The next time he woke up, it was 7:55 a.m., and his first class was a five-minute dash across campus.

Now please don't misunderstand. Alan really believed in the importance of getting dressed in the morning—and shaving and brushing his teeth and combing his hair. But there simply wasn't time. The teacher of his 8:00 class would not have excused his absence or tardiness, and furthermore, he had a quiz that morning. So, much as he hated to do it, Alan jumped up from bed, grabbed his books and papers and rushed out the door. He slid into his seat just as the final bell rang.

Have you ever met Alan? I've spent most of my life in or around the classroom; the first sixteen years as a student, followed by at least sixteen more years as a part-time teacher. I've seen thousands of students, and never once has a student come to class in his pajamas! Somehow, no matter how busy they are, no matter how late they get up in the morning, no matter how important the class, they have been able, one and all, to adjust their schedules in such a way as to show up fully dressed!

Yet not only students, but older people as well, claim time and time again that they can't have a regular devotional life with God because they don't have time.

At a medical convention in the East a few months before

writing this manuscript, I heard it again. A doctor's wife asked, in apparent sincerity, "What if you don't have time?"

We find time to dress and groom ourselves every day. We find time to eat our meals. Yet we fail to find time to put on the robe of Christ's righteousness and eat the Bread of Life. What is the problem? Is it lack of time? No. Each of us has twenty-four hours in a day. We don't lack time; we lack motivation.

When we say we don't have time for a thing, we are really saying that we don't consider it to be that important. It's still true that you have time for what you think is most important. Lack of time is not an excuse for anything, even in this world. The things you have time for are the things you value the most, and the things you do not have time for are the things you find less important It's just that simple.

Jesus pointed that out to Martha, when He was a guest in her home in Bethany. She didn't have time to sit at His feet, and she didn't think Mary had time either! Never mind the personal interview with the Son of God—the important thing in Martha's mind was to get dinner on the table! And Jesus had to remind her of what was necessary and what wasn't. "Martha, Martha, thou art careful and troubled about many things: but one thing is needful: and Mary hath chosen that good part, which shall not be taken away from her." Luke 10:41, 42.

Do you think it's your membership in the church that will insure your salvation? Do you think it's your moral behavior? Do you think it's your "working for the Lord," even while you forget the Lord of the work? Or do you believe John 17:3, that "this is life eternal, that they might know thee the only true God, and Jesus Christ, whom thou hast sent?"

We are told that "our eternal welfare depends upon the use we make during this life of our time."—*Testimonies*, vol. 5, p. 375. Yet how often have we decided by our actions that we don't have time for God?

You are invited today to a relationship and fellowship with Jesus—the one thing above all others that each one of us should have time for. If you don't have time for Him, you don't have time to live!

Thesis 49

If we don't take time for the Bible and prayer we will die spiritually.

What is the longest you have ever gone without eating? Almost everyone has probably skipped a meal here and there. How about a full 24 hours? Have you ever gone that long without food? Sometimes you have to fast that long before major surgery. What about going for 24 hours without eating when you're in good health and engaged in your usual activities? Have you ever done that?

The Bible says that Jesus and Moses went for 40 days without eating. It also records that God sustained them in a special way during that time. It's safe to say that for most of us, even to fast for 24 hours at a stretch is probably unusual.

When I was working my way through college, the cafeteria had a certain monthly minimum charge per student. If you ate more, you paid more. But if you ate less, you still paid the minimum.

One month I determined to eat less than the minimum, so I wouldn't have to pay more. For one whole week during that month, I didn't eat at all! I drank juice, nothing else. Not only was I able to continue my regular activities, I wasn't even particularly hungry.

Suppose I had decided after that one-week experiment that the way to make it through college on as little money as possible would be to continue that pattern through the entire four years? It wouldn't have been long before they would have been picking me up off the sidewalk and taking me to the hospital, would it?

161

In John 6, Jesus compared the spiritual life of communion and relationship with Him to the physical life. He said, "Except ye eat the flesh of the Son of man, and drink his blood, ye have no life in you." Verse 53. Just as it is a law in the physical life, so it is in the spiritual life: If you do not eat, you will die. It may not happen overnight, either physically or spiritually. But the law is nonetheless sure for all of that. The end result will be inevitable.

Mrs. White has told us that "it would be well for us to spend a thoughtful hour each day in contemplation of the life of Christ. We should take it point by point, and let the imagination grasp each scene, especially the closing ones."—*The Desire of Ages*, p. 83. That's the prescription for a well-balanced spiritual diet. When our spiritual food is centered on the life of Christ, we will grow.

Prayer has been called the "breath of the soul." And that draws the line even closer. You may be able to go for a day without eating, but no one can go for a day without breathing!

So when I speak of a relationship with Christ, I'm not talking about a luxury that will benefit you if you happen to have the time or the inclination to take advantage of it. I'm talking about life and death. If you do not eat or breathe spiritually, you will die. It is only through continuing fellowship and communion with Christ that spiritual life continues.

Thesis 50

Just because you read the Bible and pray doesn't mean you'll have a relationship with God. But if you don't, you won't.

Whenever a discussion comes up about the devotional life of the Christian and the importance of spending time day by day with God in His Word and in prayer, someone always asks, "Isn't it possible for the devotional life to become just another works trip?"

Before I attempt to answer that question, maybe I should define "works trip." When someone asks about the devotional life becoming just another system of works, what do they mean? Are they talking about earning or meriting salvation by putting in so much time in Bible study and prayer? It could be a real mistake to end up with some kind of righteousness by devotional life, instead of righteousness by faith in Jesus.

Perhaps we should say it here again that righteousness comes by faith in Jesus Christ alone. Period. Nothing that we do can earn or merit our salvation.

But we must accept salvation in order to benefit from it, or the entire world, including the devil and his angels, would eventually be saved. Jesus' sacrifice was enough; it was sufficient for the salvation of the entire world. But not all will accept.

Neither is salvation accepted once and for all—it must be accepted daily. The purpose of coming to Christ on a daily basis is to accept anew His grace and power and salvation. It includes much more than that, as we will notice in Thesis 95. But it includes a continuing acceptance of salvation. So it is not a matter of merit; it is a matter of method.

But the question— "Isn't it possible for the devotional life to be just another system of works?"—has another dimension. And that has to do with whether it is easy, spontaneous, and automatic, or whether there is work involved. The devotional life is not a matter of works, but it *is* work! That's an important distinction.

Many things in the Christian life are gifts. And you don't work for a gift. Faith is a gift and repentance is a gift and victory is a gift and salvation is a gift. But there is one thing that is *not* a gift. God has never promised to seek Himself for us. He has never promised to accept Himself for us. He has never promised to get acquainted with Himself for us.

All of the Christian life is not spontaneous. At times it may be a joy to seek Jesus for personal fellowship and communion. Other times it may take every ounce of willpower and self-discipline and grit and determination that you possess. Paul calls it the "fight of faith." 1 Timothy 6:12. We do not believe in a passive religion. Man has a part to accomplish in cooperating with God for his recovery, in working out his own salvation.

What a tragedy that so many Christians have misunderstood this truth. We have put forth endless time and energy and willpower trying to force ourselves to do that which we cannot do and which God has promised to do for us. And we have not done the one thing He has invited us to do—seek Him. We have waited to be "in the mood," we have waited for the devotional experience to come to us spontaneously.

If you have ever tried to spend regular time with God, you know that it can be hard work. Have you ever found yourself watching the clock to see how much time you have left? Have you ever looked ahead in that chapter you are reading to see how many more pages there are? Have you ever found it hard to pray? What do you do when this happens?

Well, one thing is for sure—quitting doesn't help. As someone has said, "When it's hardest to pray, pray the hardest." *Thoughts from the Mount of Blessing*, page 115, says, "When we feel that we have sinned and cannot pray, it is then the time to pray." So at the times you find the devotional life to be uphill business, the one thing you never do is quit.

Reading the Bible and praying is not a guarantee of spiritual life and health. It is possible to do both and still keep the heart far from God. The Pharisees did it. And so can you. But one thing is certain: You cannot maintain spiritual life if you don't seek Jesus through His Word and through prayer. Just because you eat and breathe doesn't guarantee a healthy physical life. But you won't be healthy if you don't.

Are there problems in continuing the devotional life? Sure there are. There are problems in continuing the physical life. The air is polluted. There are germs in the food. But no problem is so severe that it makes eating and breathing optional. Spiritual life can continue only as we continue to seek Him.

Thesis 51

The primary purpose of prayer is not to get answers but to know Jesus.

Think for a minute about one of your best friends. That should be a pleasant assignment! Let your mind go back to the last time you were together. What did you talk about? What did you do? How did you spend the time?

Now consider two things. First, how much of your time together did you spend asking your friend's forgiveness? And how much of your time together did you spend in asking for favors?

Do you sometimes need to ask forgiveness of a good friend? Sure. Do you ever ask your friends for favors? Sure you do. But if that were the entire basis of the relationship, it wouldn't last very long, would it?

God invites us to make friends with Him. Jesus said in John 15:14, 15: "Ye are my friends. . . . Henceforth I call you not servants; for the servant knoweth not what his lord doeth: but I have called you friends." *Steps to Christ*, page 93, says, "Prayer is the opening of the heart to God as to a friend."

God is good at giving and forgiving. He has invited us to ask. He delights to give. "It is a part of God's plan to grant us, in answer to the prayer of faith, that which He would not bestow did we not thus ask."—*The Great Controversy*, p. 525. God is not pushy, even with His blessings. He has filled His Word with promises to encourage us in coming to Him. By waiting for us to ask for His promised blessings, He is honoring our power of choice.

But we have sometimes become so involved with asking and receiving that we have forgotten how much more is available.

167

God wants more than simply to supply our needs. He wants our love.

He has given us "exceeding great and precious promises," (2 Peter 1:4), but He has never given us the assurance that every promise in the Bible is for us, at this time, and under these circumstances. The promises for spiritual blessing we can always claim. It is always His will to forgive our sin, to give us power for obedience and power for working in His service. But when it comes to the promise of temporal blessings—even life itself—we must submit our will to His will and accept His choice for us. The Bible contains promises both for deliverance and for the strength to be faithful unto death. It's God's department to decide which gift is appropriate for each need.

Does this mean that we shouldn't even ask for temporal blessings? No, it is always right to ask. God has asked us to ask! Right in the middle of the Lord's prayer is a request for a temporal blessing, "Give us this day our daily bread." "In teaching us to ask every day for what we need—both temporal and spiritual blessings—God has a purpose to accomplish for our good. He would have us realize our dependence upon His constant care, for He is seeking to draw us into communion with Himself."—*Thoughts From the Mount of Blessing*, p. 113.

Notice *why* He invites us to ask, instead of just giving us the spiritual and temporal blessings we need without our asking. It is to teach us dependence upon Him and to bring us into communion with Him.

God is not the kind of friend who talks only about His own interests. He invites us to come and talk to Him about what is on our minds. He wants to hear about what we're thinking and feeling. He wants to share with us our joys and sorrows.

Sometimes people ask, "Doesn't God already know all about us?" Of course He does! But even in human relationships, talking just for the sake of talking is important. Even on a human level, information is not nearly so important as the communication that happens when people share.

Suppose you have a close friend who gets some good news. Maybe you read about his good news in the paper, and since you know him and know something about his dreams and goals and personality, you say to yourself, "My friend will be really happy."

Then suppose he calls you on the phone and says, "Guess what!"

"No need to talk about it, my friend, I already know. I saw it in the paper, and I know you're excited. So much for that. Now let's talk about something else." Is that how you respond?

No, you listen to him tell it. You share his excitement with him. You are honored that he came to share this with you, for it is a statement of love and friendship.

God has all the information He needs. It's the fellowship with those He loves that is lacking. That's why He has invited us to share our lives with Him.

Thesis 52

The primary purpose of Bible study is not to get information but to know Jesus.

A group of Christian believers in the South Sea Islands go down to the beach every morning to look to the east to see if Jesus is coming yet. They haven't heard that God doesn't raise the dead anymore, as He did in Bible times. So they pray, and the dead are raised.

One of these Christians was trying to get the chief of the tribe to allow his daughter to be baptized. The daughter had accepted Christ, but her father had forbidden her to join the church.

"If God sends an earthquake tomorrow afternoon at three o'clock will you let your daughter be baptized?" the Christian asked the chief.

The chief agreed.

The next afternoon at three o'clock there was a tremendous earthquake, and the chief allowed his daughter to join the church.

This Christian worker was interviewed by someone here in the United States, who asked him, "Why an earthquake? Couldn't you have asked for something less spectacular?"

And the Christian from the South Sea Islands replied, "Well, can't God do anything? Why not ask for something big?"

We smile at the simple faith of these "Fuzzy Wuzzies." We smile at the faith of a little child. But we're envious as well. With all of our sophisticated information about God, sometimes we trust Him far less.

I'm not saying that information is unimportant. God has provided us with information about Himself. He wants an intelligent faith. But information is never enough. *The Desire of Ages*, page 455, makes this comment: "The perception and appreciation of truth . . . depends less upon the mind than upon the heart. Truth must be received into the soul; it claims the homage of the will. If truth could be submitted to the reason alone, pride would be no hindrance in the way of its reception."

The devil has more information about God than any of us. Yet that information was not enough to keep him from starting this whole mess in the first place. It's not enough to change his life today. He chose to rebel in the first place. He chose to rebel in the full light of God's glory, with complete information about God and His character. And all the information he possessed was not sufficient to prevent his downfall.

Information is important to communication. But information is not a substitute for communication.

Sometimes two people from different cultures will meet. It often happens during wartime when soldiers are overseas. It happens with exchange students and student missionaries. A young man and a young woman will be attracted to each other and begin a relationship. But they can't talk to each other.

They smile a lot and hold hands and kiss, and conclude that because it's pleasant to spend time together that they are communicating. He thinks she is just what he's been looking for. She thinks he is the answer to her dreams.

But sometimes after they have been together for a while, maybe even after they have married, they discover that they have nothing whatsoever in common except smiling and holding hands and kissing! Their backgrounds are different, their tastes are different, their ideas about the role of husband and wife are different, their goals for life are different. And the problems begin.

Information and communication must go together. One of the first things that happens when missionaries bring some heathen in the darkness of idolatry to Christ, is that they begin to teach them *about* Christ. We've probably all heard stories of people whom the Holy Spirit brings to an acceptance of God before the human missionary ever reaches them. But the first thing that usually happens is that the person is directed to the church, to the Word of God to gain information about God that will keep his faith alive.

On the other hand, in the so-called enlightened countries, information about God has saturated our consciousness from babyhood. But we're short on understanding about communication. We can talk until midnight about some intellectual detail and talk about God every week in Sabbath School, and yet never take the time to talk to God and communicate with Him personally.

The Bible provides information as a springboard for communication. John 17:3 says, "This is life eternal, that they might know thee." Knowing *about* God has value only as it leads to knowing Him. It is knowing Him that brings life.

Thesis 53

Things often go worse when we pray until we learn to seek Jesus for His sake, not ours.

A student told me one time, "I quit being a Christian two weeks ago, and I haven't even sinned since!"

On the other hand, many who determine to begin seeking a personal relationship with God discover that everything goes wrong. "Many who sincerely consecrate their lives to God's service are surprised and disappointed to find themselves, as never before, confronted by obstacles and beset by trials and perplexities. They pray for Christlikeness of character, for a fitness for the Lord's work, and they are placed in circumstances that seem to call forth all the evil of their nature. Faults are revealed of which they did not even suspect the existence. Like Israel of old they question, 'If God is leading us, why do all these things come upon us?' "—*The Ministry of Healing* p. 470.'

Sometimes it is hard to accept the inspired answer given in the same context, that "it is *because* God is leading them that these things come upon them. Trials and obstacles are the Lord's chosen methods of discipline and His appointed conditions of success."—*Ibid.*, p. 471. (Emphasis supplied.)

The story of Job is a strange story. Here was a man who was perfect. God said he was perfect. He said to Satan, "Hast thou considered my servant Job, that there is none like him in the earth, a perfect and an upright man, one that feareth God, and escheweth evil?" Job 1:8.

Yet God gave the devil permission to attack Job, even though Job was perfect. And overnight poor Job was faced with more problems than most people face in a lifetime. His wealth disap-

175

peared, his health disappeared, his children disappeared. More than that, he lost the respect of his wife, his reputation in the community, and the trust of his friends.

What was the devil's charge against God in this setting? He accused God of unfairly protecting Job. He accused God of being the sort of Being that had to bribe His creatures to love. He said in essense, "Job serves You only for what he can get out of You."

But God knew better! He knew what made Job tick. And so He placed His reputation on the line, before the universe, in the person of His servant Job. He said to the devil, "Go ahead and try to prove your point."

Sometimes people have objected to the story of Job, feeling that God was using Job as a pawn in His game with the devil. But it wasn't Job who was on trial—it was *God* who was on trial. And Job, who not only at the beginning didn't understand what was going on, but who was *never* given an explanation so far as the Bible records, vindicated God before the watching worlds!

Nobody admires a mercenary. We can understand the problems that the wealthy or public figures have in forming true friendships. It's not always easy to tell who wants to be friends with you as a person, or who is only trying to get something out of you.

With every person who leaves his ranks to join God's side, the devil accuses God all over again. He says, "This one is not coming to You because he loves You. He is not accepting Your service out of gratitude for what Your Son did for him. He wants his problems solved. He wants his ulcers healed. He wants peace of mind. He wants to escape the fires of judgment."

In a sense, every soul who makes a decision to accept Christ renews the great controversy. And the only way God can be vindicated, the only way He can accept our choice for Him, is if He gives the devil an opportunity to talk us out of that choice!

One student told me, "If I could know that I was saved, that my sins were forgiven, and that I was accepted by God right now, then I would want someone to kill me quick!"

"Why?"

"Because I would be afraid I would blow it!"

But God doesn't want people who come to Him only in a moment of extreme pressure and who would change their minds about wanting to belong to Him if they had half a chance. He wants our free choice. And in order to give us complete freedom of choice, He has to allow the enemy to do his best to get us to change our minds.

Not too many years ago, the United States legislated a "cooling off" period after the signing of any major contract. Even the government makes allowance for second thoughts and guarantees the right to change our minds. The choice that can outlast the bad times, as well as the good times, is the only free choice that God and the devil can both accept.

Thesis 54

Anyone who gets discouraged with his relationship because of his behavior is a legalist.

What is a legalist? Well, according to the popular definition, a legalist is anyone who hopes to gain heaven by keeping the law. The heathen or the atheist would not be a legalist, because he is not seeking salvation at all. But anyone with any hope of salvation who is basing that hope upon his own good works or his own obedience or his own merit in any way is a legalist.

The basic truth of salvation by faith alone in Jesus Christ is that we can do nothing to earn or merit our salvation. We can only accept it as a gift. And we accept it by coming into the presence of the Giver. We have talked about the fact that the gift of salvation has to be accepted day by day, and not just once and for all at the beginning of the Christian life.

Yet we hear it over and over again, "I've tried the devotional life, and it didn't work for me."

I ask, "What do you mean? Weren't you able to become better acquainted with Jesus by spending time in studying His life? Did you find that spending time in the Word of God and in prayer didn't lead you to communication with God? Did you decide that the effort involved to set aside that thoughtful hour with Him day by day wasn't worth it? *What* didn't work?"

Almost inevitably the answer is: "I found I still had to struggle with temptation. I still made some of the same mistakes I had made before. I tried a relationship with God, and it didn't work."

Jesus said, "So is the kingdom of God, as if a man should cast seed into the ground; and should sleep, and rise night and day,

179

and the seed should spring and grow up, he knoweth not how. For the earth bringeth forth fruit of herself; first the blade, then the ear, after that the full corn in the ear." Mark 4:26-28.

We don't expect to grow a garden or rear children or get an education or succeed in a new business venture or learn to play a musical instrument or construct a building overnight. But how many of us expect to become Christians instantly? How many of us are unwilling to wait for the development of the fruit of the Spirit in our lives?

Christ's Object Lessons, page 61, tells us, " 'The husbandman waiteth for the precious fruit of the earth, and hath long patience for it, until he receive the early and latter rain.' James 5:7. So the Christian is to wait with patience for the fruition in his life of the word of God. Often when we pray for the graces of the Spirit, God works to answer our prayers by placing us in circumstances to develop these fruits; but we do not understand His purpose, and wonder, and are dismayed. Yet none can develop these graces except through the process of growth and fruit bearing. Our part is to receive God's word and to hold it fast, yielding ourselves fully to its control, and its purpose in us will be accomplished."

Relationship is not based on behavior. And if it is our behavior that causes us to become discouraged with our relationship, then we know that we have been in some way counting on our behavior for acceptance with God. Anyone who expects to be accepted and saved by his own works in any way is a legalist.

Any victory over sin or power for obedience or overcoming of temptation is never going to come from within us. If we ever hope to obey, we must come to Jesus for His righteousness and keep coming to Him. The one thing you should *never* do, if you find yourself a defeated Christian, is to quit the relationship; for it is only through Christ that you can ever hope to succeed in the Christian life.

Steps to Christ, page 64, should be written in the flyleaf of every Bible. "We shall often have to bow down and weep at the feet of Jesus because of our shortcomings and mistakes, but we are not to be discouraged. Even if we are overcome by the enemy, we are not cast off, not forsaken and rejected of God. No; Christ is at the right hand of God, who also maketh intercession for us. Said the beloved John, 'These things write I unto you, that ye sin not. And if any man sin, we have an advocate with the Father, Jesus Christ the righteous.' "

Is victory and overcoming possible? Yes, God's power is available. What happens if we sin? We have the offer of forgiveness and restoration.

We may become discouraged with our behavior because of our behavior! But if we are looking to Jesus for salvation and forgiveness and power to obey, we should never become discouraged with our relationship because of our behavior. His promise is sure. If we stay with Him, He will finish His work in our lives.

Thesis 55

True obedience is a gift from God (the robe is free!).

Obedience is a gift. Obedience is a gift. Obedience is a gift. Obedience is a gift. Obedience is a gift. Obedience is a gift. Obedience is a gift. Obedience is a gift!

Obedience is a gift because faith is a gift. Review the theses on faith, if you are still in doubt about the truth that faith is a gift. Colossians 2:6 tells us, "As ye have therefore received Christ Jesus the Lord, so walk ye in him." Romans 1:17 says, "The just shall *live* by faith." (Emphasis supplied.) *Patriarchs and Prophets*, page 657, says, "Every failure on the part of the children of God is due to their lack of faith." If we come to Christ by faith in the first place, if we continue to walk with Him by faith, if our every failure is due to our lack of faith, if we are to *live* by faith, then faith is the basis for obedience. If faith is a gift, then obedience must also be a gift.

Obedience is a gift because of the nature of mankind. Review the theses on sin if you have any doubt about the fallen nature of mankind. Romans 5:12 tells us that "all have sinned." *Steps to Christ*, page 18, says, "Our hearts are evil, and we cannot change them." If we are sinful by nature, if our hearts are evil, then how could *we* ever produce obedience? Any genuine righteousness in our lives must come from outside ourselves. The Lord is our righteousness. See Jeremiah 23:6. If we have no righteousness and the Lord is the only One who has righteousness, then whatever righteousness we experience must be a gift from Him.

Obedience is a gift because surrender is a gift. Review the theses on surrender if you wonder about this one. Romans 10:3 says of Israel, "For they being ignorant of God's righteousness, and going about to establish their own righteousness, have not submitted themselves unto the righteousness of God." Do you want your own righteousness, which is described as filthy rags? Or do you want the righteousness of God? To obtain *His* righteousness, you must submit or surrender yourself to Him. If surrender is a gift, then the obedience that comes as a result of that surrender would have to be a gift as well.

Obedience is a gift because of God's control. Review theses 20 and 21 for this one. If we give up our power of choice to God and accept His control in place of the devil's control, then *He* is the one who is working in us to will and to do of His good pleasure. See Philippians 2:13. "Every soul that refuses to give himself to God is under the control of another power."—*The Desire of Ages*, p. 466. We are controlled by either God or the devil. When God is in control, He gives us His gifts of righteousness and obedience. As long as God is in control, we will be genuinely obedient.

Obedience is a gift because of the Sabbath rest. We haven't covered the ground on this one yet. But Ezekiel 20:12, 20 tells us that the Sabbath is a sign of sanctification. Hebrews 4 describes a rest that remains for the people of God—a rest symbolized by the Sabbath rest. "He that is entered into his rest, he also hath ceased from his own works, as God did from his." Verse 10. How do we obtain this rest? Jesus says, "Come unto me, . . . and I will give you rest." Matthew 11:28. If the Sabbath rest is a symbol of our rest from working to produce our own sanctification, then obedience would be a gift, because rest is a gift.

Obedience is a gift because repentance is a gift. Review the section on repentance if you have any question about repentance being a gift. Repentance includes sorrow for sin and turning away from it. If repentance is a gift, then sorrow for sin is a gift, and turning away from sin is a gift.

Obedience is a gift because fruit is a gift. Fruit is natural and spontaneous. And Jesus longs for fruit from His children. He talks about fruit at length in John 15. "Yet the Saviour does not bid the disciples labor to bear fruit. He tells them to abide in Him."—*The Desire of Ages*, p. 677. The labor is in abiding in Him, *not* in trying to produce fruit. And "obedience is the fruit of faith."—*Steps to Christ*, p. 61. Therefore, since fruit is a gift, obedience is a gift.

Obedience is a gift because of the example of Jesus. For a more detailed explanation of this point, look ahead to the last section, the one about Jesus. How did Jesus obey? *The Desire of ages*, page 24: "As the Son of man, He gave us an example of obedience; as the Son of God, He gives us power to obey." Jesus said, "I can of mine own self do nothing." He also said, "without me ye can do nothing." If His obedience came as a gift from His Father, then our obedience must come as a gift from Him. It is good news that obedience is a gift!

Thesis 56

Real obedience comes from the inside out, not from the outside in.

When my brother and I were small, our mother sewed chef hats and aprons for us and gave us jobs helping her in the kitchen. One of our jobs was to wash the dishes, and we would take turns. One time my brother would wash and I would dry; another time I would wash, and he would dry.

Those dishes were exceptionally clean by the time we got through with them, because nothing brought greater joy to the heart of the one drying than to be able to return a dish to be rewashed! My brother would hand a dish back to me, and I would say, "That dish is clean!"

He would point to some tiny spot that had been missed and say, "You call *that* clean?" And back into the suds it went.

One thing I learned during my apprenticeship in the kitchen: If you get the inside clean, the outside is going to be clean too.

Jesus once used the same analogy to rebuke the Pharisees. He said, "Woe unto you, scribes and Pharisees, hypocrites! for ye make clean the outside of the cup and of the platter, but within they are full of extortion and excess. Thou blind Pharisee, cleanse first that which is within the cup and platter, that the outside of them may be clean also." Matthew 23:25, 26.

When God works on the sin problem, He goes to the heart of the matter—the heart of the person! This is one of the major premises of righteousness by faith. God is not in the business of putting bandaids on cancer. He knows that when the heart is right, everything else will fall into place.

We human beings are impressed with external obedience, because the outside is all we can see. But God looks upon the heart, and no amount of external polishing can disguise the sin that is in the heart. Therefore only the cleansing of the heart has any value in His estimation.

A classic paragraph on this subject, written to our church a long time ago, shows up, of all places, in the book *Counsels on Diet and Foods*. "The plan of beginning outside and trying to work inward has always failed, and always will fail. God's plan with you is to begin at the very seat of all difficulties, the heart, and then from out of the heart will issue the principles of righteousness; the reformation will be outward as well as inward."— Page 35.

There is a philosophy in the world today that you can find at every turn. It says that the way to change is to fake it on the outside for a period of time, and that if you continue to fake it long enough, the change will finally be internalized. For instance, suppose you hate your neighbor. Well, if you will just *act* in a loving way, sooner or later you will begin to love him. The same for a failing marriage: just act as though you're in love again, and soon everything will be solved. If you're having a problem with weight, just act like a thin person, and soon you will be thin. If you're having financial problems, just act like a millionaire, and first thing you know, you'll be wealthy!

Positive thinking has been around for a long time. There's just one problem with it—it doesn't work. Lucifer was the first one who tried it; he said to himself, "I will be like God." And he began trying to act like God, and ended up acting like the devil! Yet how many Christians have tried his method, hoping to act like God, act like Jesus, behave in a loving way? It's a dead-end street.

On the other hand, if you allow God to work His miracle in your heart and change you on the inside, the outside will inevitably reflect that inner transformation. The inner change is available. It comes through beholding Him and allowing His Spirit to change the heart.

Thesis 57

Genuine obedience is natural and spontaneous. It comes only through the faith relationship with Christ.

Have you ever heard of a "contradiction in terms"? English language experts have a fancy word for it, but what they are talking about is the use of two words together that contradict each other. An example would be "cruel kindness," or "brave coward." Sometimes writers or speakers might use some such contradiction in terms to try to describe two conflicting emotions or events.

What about "natural obedience"? Does that sound to you like a contradiction in terms? When you think of obedience, do you think of hard work, effort, and struggle? Is it possible for obedience to be natural?

One reason why obedience might not be natural would be if that obedience were only external, and not internal. If you want to do one thing but force yourself to do something else, then obedience would not be spontaneous.

How much of our so-called obedience has been forcing ourselves to do something we don't want to do? We do it as children. Our parents tell us to clean our rooms or take a bath or eat the spinach. But we like our rooms the way they are. We're at the stage of being allergic to water. We hate spinach. And so we balk and complain and finally grudgingly do what we're forced to do. And we come to think of that as obedience.

It can be tremendous good news to discover that God has a better plan for obedience than that! *The Acts of the Apostles*, pages 482, 483, describes it: "Of ourselves, we are not able to bring the purposes and desires and inclinations into harmony with the will of God; but if we are 'willing to be made willing,' the Saviour will accomplish this for us, 'Casting down imaginations, and every high thing that exalteth itself against the knowledge of God, and bringing into captivity every thought to the obedience of Christ.' 2 Corinthians 10:5."

If your thoughts and desires are for the right, then won't the natural and spontaneous thing be to follow through with the right actions?

God has promised some exciting changes in our thinking, which will result in genuine obedience instead of outward conformity. He has promised to bring our feelings, our thoughts, and our purposes into harmony with His will. See *Steps to Christ*, p. 61. He has promised to change the tastes and inclinations until they are pure and holy. See *Gospel Workers*, p. 127. He has promised to bring the thoughts and desires into obedience to the will of Christ. See *The Desire of Ages*, p. 176. He has promised that by looking to Jesus, by beholding Him, we will become changed until goodness becomes our natural instinct. See *Christ's Object Lessons*, p. 355. He promises to give us a new mind, new purposes, and new motives. See *Messages to Young People*, p. 72.

Think about it for a moment. If your feelings, thoughts, purposes, tastes, inclinations, desires, motives, and instincts are in harmony with the will and mind of God, then what will happen to your actions? Will you have to work hard to obey, or will you find obedience natural and spontaneous?

Notice these paragraphs. "If we have the love of Christ in our souls, it will be a natural consequence for us to have all the other graces—joy, peace, long-suffering, gentleness, goodness, faith, meekness, temperance."—*My Life Today*, p. 50. "The children of God never forget to do good. . . . Good works are spontaneous with them, for God has transformed their natures by His grace."—*Ibid.*, p. 193.

To describe obedience as "natural" and "spontaneous" is not a contradiction in terms. It is good news! God's plan for you is to change you from the inside out, so that obeying Him will bring you the greatest delight, because it is exactly what you feel like doing.

Thesis 58

One who is depending on God for power doesn't have to try hard to obey. He would have to try hard not to.

My brother and I were roommates in college. This surprised our parents, because my brother and I had fought so much when we were younger that our parents sometimes wondered if we would live to grow up—much less ever become good friends! But the miracle finally happened, and we shared the same room by choice.

One Saturday night my brother was restless. It was the middle of the winter—the terrible kind of winter they have in southern California—fog! It was an ideal night for staying indoors, propping your feet up on the desk, and relaxing with a good book.

My brother, however, decided to take a walk instead. In fact, he decided to walk to Glendale, seventy-five miles away!

This was not a rational decision! Under normal circumstances, the kind thing to do would have been to tie him up somewhere until sanity returned. But my brother had a fiancée in Glendale. He was in love. And I knew about his disease! So not only did I not try to stop him, I even went so far as to consider his actions excusable!

We have noticed so far in this section that obedience is a gift. We have seen how true obedience comes from the inside out, not the outside in. We have understood that genuine obedience is natural and spontaneous. Now we're going to go even one step farther: If you are experiencing genuine obedience, you would have to try harder *not* to obey than you would to obey.

If you have trouble with that premise, remember my brother

191

walking to Glendale! He was motivated by the most powerful force in the world, the power of love. In spite of the circumstances, in spite of the obstacles, in spite of the distance, it would have been much harder for him to stay in his dormitory room than to walk the seventy-five miles. Walking to Glendale was easy compared to sitting with his feet on the desk, reading a good book. Hitchhiking in the fog was easy compared to staying indoors. Going to Glendale was the natural and spontaneous thing for him to do.

Sometimes people become afraid that when we talk about natural and spontaneous obedience, we are talking about effortless obedience. Is there effort involved in obeying God? Sure there is! Was there effort involved for my brother to walk to Glendale? Of course! But the crucial issue is: Wherein lies the greater effort?

If it is harder for you to obey God than to follow your own impulses, then you are not experiencing natural obedience yet. If it would be harder for you to disobey, because your own impulse is to obey God, then you can know that God is working in you, to will and do of His good pleasure.

In Psalm 40:8, David described natural obedience when he said, "I delight to do thy will, O my God: yea, thy law is within my heart." "Looking unto Jesus we obtain brighter and more distinct views of God, and by beholding we become changed. Goodness, love for our fellow men, becomes our natural instinct."—*Christ's Object Lessons,* p. 355.

If it is your natural instinct to obey, if God's law is within your heart and you find delight in doing His will, then you would have to try harder to disobey than to obey.

That doesn't mean that obedience is always easy. It is not always easy to follow your natural instincts! Take the example of a mother caring for her child. Her natural instincts lead her to place the needs of the child above her own needs. Her natural instincts will lead her to change the baby's diapers, even though I can assure you from personal experience that changing diapers is not always a pleasant task! Her natural instincts will cause her to get up in the middle of the night to feed and care for her baby when she would really be much more comfortable asleep in bed. Is caring for a baby always easy? No, but it is the natural thing for a mother or father who loves.

For the one who is controlled by God, obedience may not always be easy. But it is always *easiest!*

Thesis 59

Obedience that is only external is false obedience.

Children are notorious for blurting out whatever is in their minds, greeting a dinner guest by announcing, "My mother says she hopes you don't talk about your operation while we're trying to eat" or asking Aunt Minnie, "Why are your teeth so crooked?"

We older people cringe and try to explain the difference between being tactful and being dishonest! It's not always an easy distinction.

Teenagers often complain about hypocrites in the church. They are quick to discern a double standard in their teachers and leaders. Sometimes their questions can make us even more uncomfortable than the blunt observations of a five-year-old. But they demand straight answers and despise pretension. One expression I heard recently from the teenage set was, "Get *real!*"

It was used as a challenge to reality, meaning the same thing as, "You've got to be kidding!" or "You're putting me on!" or "You don't really mean that!"

God Himself likes reality! When Jesus was here, He came down harder on the Pharisees than on anyone else. Some of the strongest language in the Bible is addressed to the hypocrites, such as Revelation 3, where God goes so far as to say that He prefers the open sinner to the pretend Christian. Only He wasn't that "polite" about saying it! "I know thy works, that thou art neither cold nor hot: I would thou wert cold or hot. So then because thou art lukewarm, and neither cold nor hot, I will spue thee out of my mouth." Verses 15, 16. "Your self-righteousness is nauseating to the Lord Jesus Christ."—Ellen G. White Comments, *S.D.A. Bible Commentary,* vol. 7, p. 963.

God insists on reality! He wants only prayer that comes from the heart. He doesn't want just the words. See *Thoughts from the Mount of Blessing,* p. 86. He wants only the gifts and offerings that come because of love and a willingness to give. He doesn't want anything that is given grudgingly. See 2 Corinthians 9:7. And He wants only the service of love. He wants obedience that comes from the heart.

External obedience doesn't count with God. "There are those who profess to serve God, while they rely upon their own efforts to obey His law, to form a right character, and secure salvation. Their hearts are not moved by any deep sense of the love of Christ, but they seek to perform the duties of the Christian life as that which God requires of them in order to gain heaven. *Such religion is worth nothing.*"—*Steps to Christ,* p. 44. (Emphasis supplied.)

"The man who attempts to keep the commandments of God from a sense of obligation merely—because he is required to do so—will never enter into the joy of obedience. *He does not obey.* When the requirements of God are accounted a burden because they cut across human inclination, we may know that the life is not a Christian life. True obedience is the outworking of a principle within."—*Christ's Object Lessons,* p. 97. (Emphasis supplied.)

Here we find another convincing argument for "natural" obedience. God doesn't even consider "good deeds" to be obedience unless they come from the heart. Therefore, any morality that we can come up with apart from Him, any forcing ourselves to do what God has asked us to do, doesn't even count as obedience.

God recognizes only reality! If our obedience doesn't come from the inside, it's not obedience at all. That's what Jesus said in Matthew 5, when He reminded us that hate is the basis of murder and lust is the basis of adultery. It's not enough simply to refrain from the evil deed. The desire for wrong cherished in the heart is sin.

God promises us reality! He has more to offer us than a life-time of forcing ourselves to do what we hate and gritting our teeth to keep from doing what we really love. When He lives His life in us, we will obey because obedience is in harmony with our own desires. That's the only kind of genuine obedience there is.

Thesis 60

When we know God as it is our privilege to know Him, our lives will be lives of continual obedience.

A classic paragraph in the book *The Desire of Ages* sums up the question of obedience. It identifies genuine obedience; it tells us how genuine obedience can be obtained.

"All true obedience comes from the heart. It was heart work with Christ. And if we consent, He will so identify Himself with our thoughts and aims, so blend our hearts and minds into conformity to His will, that when obeying Him we shall be but carrying out our own impulses. The will, refined and sanctified, will find its highest delight in doing His service. When we know God as it is our privilege to know Him, our life will be a life of continual obedience. Through an appreciation of the character of Christ, through communion with God, sin will become hateful to us."—Page 668.

Let's go back and read it carefully, taking one sentence at a time.

"All true obedience comes from the heart." If that is true, then all obedience that does not come from the heart is not true obedience, right? If we have to work hard to obey, going against our own desires and inclinations, then whatever we manage to produce is only morality, never obedience.

"It was heart work with Christ." Christ is the greatest single example of righteousness by faith. He came to this earth not only to die for us, but also to show us how to live. Revelation 3:21 gives the promise, "To him that overcometh will I grant to sit with me in my throne, even as I also overcame, and am set down with my Father in his throne." We are invited to be overcomers in the same way in which Christ overcame.

"If we consent, He will so identify Himself with our thoughts and aims, so blend our hearts and minds into conformity to His will, that when obeying Him we shall be but carrying out our own impulses." What is our part? To consent. What is His part? To change our hearts and minds and even our impulses, until we find ourselves doing His will naturally and spontaneously. Do you like the sound of impulsive obedience? Would it be good news to you, when faced with a decision in your life, to discover that your first impulse was in harmony with the will of God? It's available!

"The will, refined and sanctified, will find its highest delight in doing His service." If the service of God was your highest delight, would you have to try hard to obey? Would obedience be hard work? Or would it be—well, delightful!

Now comes the method, the explanation for how all of this can happen in our lives. "When we know God as it is our privilege to know Him, our life will be a life of continual obedience."

Let me ask you, if you find that you are not experiencing continual obedience as yet, what is the problem? Do you need to try harder? Do you need to make more resolutions? Do you need to develop your will power? Or do you need to put forth greater effort to know God as it is your privilege to know Him?

And finally, "Through an appreciation of the character of Christ, through communion with God, sin will become hateful to us." Do you find sin hateful? Or do you sometimes find sin attractive? If you find sin attractive instead of hateful, what is wrong? You have not yet gained a true appreciation of the character of Christ; you need to commune with God.

When we become acquainted with God, knowing Him as it is our privilege to know Him, obedience will be natural, spontaneous, and impulsive! As we place our deliberate effort toward communion with Him, obedience will be the inevitable result.

Thesis 61

Anyone who tries to live the Christian life apart from Christ is not a Christian. He is a legalist, whether conservative or liberal.

Some legalists are black legalists, and some are red legalists! As we have already noticed, a legalist is one who thinks to earn salvation by keeping the law, or in any other way, apart from Christ.

A black legalist then, is one with a black suit and black tie, black shoes and black socks! He is the one with the long face. He is the conservative legalist, who finds his security in the church standards that he upholds. But he is a legalist, for he has no time for personal fellowship and acquaintance with the Lord Jesus, although he may spend a lot of time studying doctrine and standards and ethics.

A red legalist is one who wears jewelry and goes to the movies and perhaps has a glass of wine now and then. (The analogy comes from the description in Revelation 17 of the woman on the scarlet beast. She "was arrayed in purple and scarlet color, and decked with gold and precious stones and pearls." Verse 4. This is only an analogy to make a point; it is not new prophetic truth on the mysteries of the book of Revelation!) The red legalist, then, is the liberal legalist who finds security in the church standards that he has abandoned. The red legalist considers the black legalist to be a legalist, but often fails to realize that he himself is simply a legalist of a different color. For it makes no difference whether you are liberal or conservative; if you have no time to spend in personal relationship and communion with Christ, you are not a Christian.

Sometime parents ask, "But isn't it better to be a legalist than to be an open sinner? If we can teach our children to obey the law of God externally, won't that finally lead to the religion of the heart?"

It didn't for the Pharisees! They were the hardest of all for Christ to reach when He was here on this earth. The converts that they brought into the church were not only as legalistic as their teachers, but Jesus said in Matthew 23:15 that they were twofold more the children of hell than the Pharisees themselves. *The Desire of Ages*, page 280, states clearly, "A legal religion can never lead souls to Christ."

It is impossible to gain salvation by keeping the law. "He who is trying to reach heaven by his own works in keeping the law is attempting an impossibility."—*Ibid.*, 172. "Therefore by the deeds of the law there shall no flesh be justified in his sight." Romans 3:20.

Why emphasize the law, then, if keeping the law cannot save us? Why talk about it or study it at all? If our efforts to keep the law can actually prevent us from coming to Christ for salvation, wouldn't it be better not to hear about the law at all?

The law has several important and legitimate functions. The law cannot save us, but it can show us our need of salvation. The law cannot change us, but it can show us our need of change. Paul describes the law as a schoolmaster to bring us to Christ. See Galatians 3:24, 25. James calls the law a "looking glass." James 1:23-25. A mirror can show us our need of cleansing, but it cannot cleanse us. So it is with the law of God. It shows us our sinful condition in order to motivate us to go to Christ for cleansing and restoration. The law can diagnose, but it cannot treat or cure the disease of sin.

The law condemns. And when we recognize our condemnation, we realize our need for pardon. The law reveals the curse that we are under as lawbreakers, and thereby prepares us to accept the good news that Christ has redeemed us from the curse of the law. See Galatians 3:13.

And the law is a protector. The law protects the innocent. It also protects the guilty! When we come before the judgment bar of God, we can know clearly whether we are at fault. We don't have to worry that God will play favorites or judge according to His temporary whim of fancy. He has stated clearly His requirements, and thus both innocent and guilty can know where they stand. Those who have accepted the righteousness of Christ in place of their own unrighteousness can stand acquited, protected by the law that does not condemn them. The guilty will see clearly their own rejection of God's grace and will know that they have been fairly tried.

When you look into God's law, do you find that it condemns you? Then praise the Lord! The time of probation still lingers. It is not too late to allow the law to do its work in bringing you to Christ.

Thesis 62

There is no power for genuine obedience in the law. Mount Sinai is no good without Mount Calvary.

Logic alone has no power. Science has proved without a doubt that a definite link exists between smoking and lung cancer. Highway statistics continue to show that drinking and driving is extremely hazardous, not only to your health, but to the health of those around you. Sniffing glue and cocaine, swallowing "uppers" or LSD, ingesting PCP or "angel dust" have all been proved to destroy the brain and threaten life. Yet a major portion of the American public, continue to use cigarettes, alcohol, and drugs.

In spite of consumer reports proving time and time again that "junk food" has little nutritional value, the fast-food industry is one of the fastest growing around. We have proved that air pollution and water pollution threaten the very life of future generations. But we keep on using and abusing the things that cause pollution. In spite of AIDS and other social diseases, millions still practice sexual promiscuity. Knowledge is not virtue. Information is not overcoming. Facts cannot provide freedom. There is no power in logic.

When God gave His law amid the thunderings of Mount Sinai, the people of Israel were convinced of its logic and reason. "All the people answered together, and said, All that the Lord hath spoken we will do." Exodus 19:8. They were admitting that the law was just, but they had yet to learn its proper function. They had yet to learn by hard experience the truth expressed in the writings to our church, "As you look into the Lord's great moral looking glass, His holy law, His standard of character, do not for a moment suppose that it can cleanse you."—Ellen G. White Comments, *S.D.A. Bible Commentary* vol. 6, p.1070.

What was God's response to the people of Israel? You can read it in Deuteronomy 5:28-30. "The Lord heard the voice of your words, when ye spake unto me; and the Lord said unto me, I have heard the voice of the words of this people, which they have spoken unto thee: they have well said all that they have spoken." It was good that they realized that God's law was worthwhile. But it was not enough. The Lord continued, "O that there were such a heart in them, that they would fear me, and keep all my commandments always, that it might be well with them, and with their children for ever!" You can almost hear the tears in His voice as He says it. For the Lord knew something that the people of Israel had yet to learn by hard experience. He knew there was no power in logic. He knew that no one could obey the law in his own strength. But He could not explain their error to them in words they would understand and accept. He could only let them learn the hard way. You can almost hear Him sigh and see Him shake His head, and He concludes in verse 30, "Go say to them, Get you into your tents again." School was dismissed for that day! Until life itself taught them their need, all God could say to them was, "Go to your tents!"

Many parents have wondered at their erring children. Time and time again they have said, "But they *know* what is right." And the children probably do know. Our human dilemma is that knowledge is not enough. Not only do we need to know what is right, we also need to know how to do the right we know. And there's where the problem so often comes in.

God has seen our perplexity and understands our helpless condition. In His great love, He did not stop with Mount Sinai. He provides another mountain, Mount Calvary. Through accepting the righteousness of Christ in our behalf, through a continued relationship with Him, He gives us that which the people of Israel lacked—the law of God written in our hearts. Jesus can give us what the law can never give—power for obedience, pardon for sin, grace for our every need.

Thesis 63

Christ is the end of the law for righteousness, but not the end of the law.

In recent years the number of available Bible translations and paraphrases has increased markedly. Some are good; some are not so good. But often by comparing the wording of several different translations, you can gain a better understanding of what a Bible text means.

This particular version that I will use here is called the Venden Revised Version! It's a paraphrase of Romans 9:30—10:4. "What shall we say then? The Gentiles, who didn't work on producing fruit, have produced fruit—and it's the real thing too! But Israel, who worked very hard to try to produce fruit, have not managed to grow any fruit at all. Why? Because they tried to do it themselves, by working hard on the fruit. Brethren, my heart's desire and prayer to God for Israel is that they might be saved. For I bear them record that they have worked hard—but not on the right things. For they haven't understood God's way of producing fruit, so they have come up with their own way to try to grow fruit and have not submitted themselves to God's way of doing things. For Christ is the end of working hard to produce fruit for every one that believeth."

Translating the Bible is hard work! Try it sometime on a favorite passage of yours and see how you do!

What Paul is describing in Romans 9 to 10 is the misunderstanding that Israel had about how to produce the fruits of righteousness. They didn't comprehend God's methods, and so they devised their own methods which didn't work. They had put forth a lot of effort. Paul was willing to admit that. But their effort ended in nothing, because it was directed toward the wrong thing.

Two extremes of thinking seem to show up when it comes to keeping the law. The first is, "If the law is good, let's all work hard to obey it." The result is legalism and no genuine obedience. The second extreme is, if we are not supposed to work hard to keep the law, it must not be necessary to keep the law at all." The result is antinomianism and no genuine obedience. Both extremes lead to the same error in the end.

The righteousness that comes by faith in Christ alone brings good news—that genuine obedience *is* possible, but that it does not come through our own efforts to produce obedience. Correctly understanding the experience of righteousness by faith in Christ alone prevents both legalism and lawlessness.

Through an ongoing relationship and fellowship with the Lord Jesus, we realize a continually greater appreciation of His love and kindness toward us. And, "as soon as we have a correct view of the love of God, we shall have no disposition to abuse it."—*Selected Messages*, bk. 1, p. 312. Christ is not the end of the law; He is the end of our own futile efforts to keep the law. The sure result of a faith relationship with Him will be genuine lawkeeping that comes from the heart. "Good works will follow as the blossoms and fruit of faith. Appropriation of the righteousness of Christ will be manifested in a well-ordered life and godly conversation."—Ellen G. White, *Signs of the Times*, September 5, 1892.

The ultimate test of whether a person is in favor of the law of God is whether he is living in a faith relationship with Christ so that the law can be written on his heart. If we acknowledge the claims of God's law and the reality that we cannot keep the law, our only option is to come to Christ for His gift of righteousness.

Thesis 64

Good works done apart from Christ are bad works.

Below is a list of actions. Please decide which of these actions are good and which ones are bad.

1. Feeding someone who is hungry.
2. Giving someone a flower.
3. Going to church.
4. Offering a ride to a stranded traveler.
5. Smiling.
6. Visiting the sick.
7. Saying "thank you" and "please" and "I beg your pardon."
8. Taking a loaf of fresh-baked bread to a neighbor.
9. Donating money to the church.
10. Sharing your faith.

Now let me ask you, Have you ever had some young person approach you at the airport, smile, and hand you a flower? Then he wanted you to give him money, right? And if you gave him money, into whose pocket would that money disappear? It would go to the leaders of the particular cult he represented! So are smiling and giving people flowers good actions, or bad?

Consider this paragraph, found in *The Great Controversy,* page 509: "The tempter often works most successfully through those who are least suspected of being under his control. . . . The opinion prevails with many that all which appears like courtesy or refinement must, in some sense, pertain to Christ. Never was there a greater mistake. These qualities should grace the character of every Christian, for they would exert a powerful influence in favor of true religion; but they must be consecrated to God, or they are also a power for evil. Many a man of cultured intellect and pleasant manners, who would not stoop to what is commonly regarded as an immoral act, is but a polished instrument in the hands of Satan." So good manners are not proof in themselves.

Jesus said, in Matthew 7:22, 23: "Many will say to me in that day, Lord, Lord, have we not prophesied in thy name? and in thy name have cast out devils? and in thy name done many wonderful works? And then will I profess unto them, I never knew you: depart from me, ye that work iniquity." So wonderful works done apart from a relationship with Christ apart from *knowing* Christ, are called what? Iniquity.

It's possible for an atheist to bake a good loaf of bread and share it with a neighbor. Worldly people who have no time for God can be concerned about world hunger and work to relieve it. It is possible for the heathen or infidel to visit the sick. Money can be donated to the church that God will not accept. Some who attend church are Satan's agents, not children of the Lord. The Pharisees shared their faith and brought in converts who were twice as wicked as themselves. Even a desperate criminal can offer a ride to a stranded traveler and use the opportunity to take advantage of the helpless.

Good works done apart from Christ are bad works. In order for works to be *good* works, they must be done to the honor and glory of God. "Let your light so shine before men, that they may see your good works," the Saviour declared. Matthew 5:16. These "good works" will *begin* to appear when repentance and conversion take place. Not until then can words and works "glorify your Father which is in heaven."

Romans 14:23 says, "Whatsoever is not of faith is sin." When God judges, He looks upon the heart, the motives, the hidden agenda of the mind. If we are living apart from Christ, we have no choice but to be operating from a base of selfishness, and therefore our good works are not good works at all.

It is true that if a person is starving and someone gives him a loaf of bread, he will be fed regardless of the motives of the one feeding him. But so far as the individual doing the giving is concerned, any good works that he performs apart from Christ are bad works. Christ living in the heart by faith, and thus willing and doing in us, is the only source of good works.

Thesis 65

The purpose of good works is not to save us, but to bring glory to God.

At any discussion of salvation by faith in Jesus Christ alone, and of the fact that our works are in no way the basis of our salvation, someone almost always asks, "If good works do not play a part in saving us, then of what value are they?"

Matthew 5:16 is very clear: "Let your light so shine before men, that they may see your good works, and glorify your Father which is in heaven." Just because good works do not save us does not mean that good works are unimportant. The purpose of good works is to bring glory to God.

Well then, what is the purpose of bringing glory to God? Is God interested in glory because He is self-centered and egotistical? Does he ask us to be other-centered when He Himself is not? We know the answer to that question right away, because of what Jesus did at the cross. When Jesus cried, "It is finished," He answered forever Satan's accusations that God was selfish and knew nothing of self-sacrifice. The cross proved that God was willing to go the limit in giving.

So what is the purpose of bringing glory to God? One major reason is that He deserves it! He is worthy of our praise. All of the glory and honor and praise that mankind can offer to Him could never be too much. David said, "Blessed be the Lord, who daily loadeth us with benefits." Psalm 68:19. Have you been noticing your load of benefits lately? Sometimes it's easier to focus on the load of sin or the load of guilt or the load of care that we find ourselves carrying. These are loads that God never intended for us to bear. He has promised to take these loads from our shoulders and give us rest. But the one load He has for us is the load of benefits! There are a lot of them! Who could even count them all?

A second major reason for bringing glory to God is for Christian outreach and witness. As others see Jesus uplifted in our lives, and through us learn of the love and mercy of God, they are motivated to come to Him for themselves. The good works demonstrated in the life of the believer are a powerful argument in favor of Christianity, are they not?

A third major reason for bringing glory to God is that if our good works don't glorify God, whom do they glorify? Do you know the answer? There's only one other option, isn't there? If God doesn't get the glory, *we* take the glory for ourselves. And the work of justification is to lay the glory of mankind in the dust. We cannot glorify God and ourselves at the same time. Either He is glorified, or we take the honor and glory and credit for ourselves.

Which brings us to a question. Would it even be possible for someone to be saved who was not interested in bringing glory to God? Bringing glory to God should be a powerful motivation for good works. And it will be, if we serve Him because we love Him.

We find it true in our human relationships. The upholding of the family name can be a real motivation, can't it? We are willing to sacrifice many things in order to honor those we love and not disappoint them. When we know God as it is our privilege to know Him, and when we love God as it is our privilege to love Him, we will find our highest delight in honoring and glorifying Him. To obey and serve Him for His sake can be the greatest motivation of all.

"Everything is secondary to the glory of God. Our heavenly Father is to be ever cherished as the first, the joy and prosperity, the light and sufficiency of our life, and our portion forever."—*Sons and Daughters of God*, p. 56.

Thesis 66

When it comes to genuine faith and works, you can't have one without the other.

An old song says, "Love and marriage, love and marriage, go together like a horse and carriage—you can't have one without the other." (It's a *very* old song, as you can tell for more reasons than just the part about the horse and carriage!) People today have gone to a lot of trouble trying to prove that love and marriage don't necessarily have to go together. And all they have been able to prove in the process is that God's plan for marriage and family is best, after all.

But faith and works always go together. Perhaps I can find an illustration that no one could question. What about sunshine and shadow? They always go together, don't they? You can't have one without the other! In this world, whenever there is light, there is also shadow—it's an inflexible law.

Steps to Christ, page 83, speaks of the "unshadowed joy of the life to come." On this earth, even our joy is shadowed! Perhaps it's this "shadowed joy" that makes it possible to cry tears of joy. For any joy we have always comes with a shadow. We rejoice when someone accepts Christ into his life, while at the same time we feel the shadow of those who are rejecting Him. We find joy in the beauties of nature, but the shadow of death and decay is always present, no matter where we turn. Good news and bad news come together. Sometimes we will experience— as a rare gift—a "perfect" day, but there is always the shadow of the day before and the day to follow. Our human relationships are shadowed; loving acceptance from one side is coupled with misunderstanding on the other. Our hearts can burn within us when God Himself draws near to commune with us; yet there is always the shadow, even there, of times when He seemed to veil His face and we could not sense His presence.

So whether you're talking about the physical world or the spiritual, sunshine and shadow always go together.

It's the same with faith and works. If the works are genuine, their source is faith in Christ. If the faith is genuine, works will inevitably result. When you make the choice to abide in Christ, you have already made your choice about bearing fruit, for whoever abides in Him brings forth much fruit. Faith and works cannot be separated. *Selected Messages*, bk. 1, p. 397, says, "Genuine faith will be manifested in good works; for good works are the fruits of faith."

When we talk about faith and works, someone usually brings up the illustration of the two oars. Faith and works are like two oars. If you try to row with one oar—either one—you will make no progress. But if you use both oars together, your boat will go forward toward the heavenly shore! And the person using the illustration usually does so to try to prove that we should put forth equal effort on both faith and works.

But the truth is that we are not to work on either! Faith is a gift, and obedience is a gift. What we should work on is staying in the boat—or staying in relationship with Christ through prayer and the study of His Word. When we come to Christ for fellowship and communion with Him, the first byproduct is genuine faith. And the second is genuine righteousness.

The illustration of the oars is a valid one, however, if you understand it correctly—that faith and works are like two oars in terms of importance. Faith and works are equally important. But the method for obtaining both faith and works is through an ongoing relationship with Jesus Christ.

In James 2:17, we find it is possible to have dead faith. James says, "Faith, if it hath not works, is dead, being alone." In Hebrews 6:1, we find it is possible to have dead works as well. Faith *and* works must both be present in order for either one to remain alive. Genuine works will follow genuine faith, and genuine faith will come as a result of communion with God, as surely as sunshine is followed by shadow.

GROWTH

Thesis 67

Faith grows in quantity, not quality. Growth is in the constancy of dependence upon God.

Martha had finally come out of the kitchen! She had learned for herself what it was to sit at Jesus' feet with Mary. She believed that Jesus was the Messiah, the Saviour of the world, the Sent of God. She believed that whatever He requested from the Father would be granted. She accepted His claim to be the Resurrection and the Life. But when the eyes of all those people fastened upon her brother's silent tomb and Jesus asked that the stone be removed, Martha's faith wavered. On-again, off-again Martha.

Abraham was God's special friend. He had left his home and country to become a wanderer, following the inner Voice that directed his ways. The objections of his family and friends had not swayed him from his choice. When God promised him a son, an heir, to be the father of a great multitude, he had rejoiced. But one thing he had never expected: he didn't know it would take so much time. The waiting was what proved to be too much. He ended up being the father of *two* multitudes, each warring against the other to the present time. On-again, off-again Abraham.

Moses was a prophet and more than a prophet. He had spoken with God face to face. For forty years he had led a rebellious, stubborn people across the desert wastes, ministering to their varied necessities. He had defended them to God Himself, refusing to agree to their destruction even when they richly deserved it. Yet his faith failed on the very borders of the Land of Promise, and he sinned so publicly and so unmistakably that

God had no choice but to deny him the privilege of finishing the job he had started. On-again, off-again Moses.

The on-again, off-again club has many members! David, Samson, Adam, Paul, Hezekiah, Peter, Jacob. The list could go on and on. Sacred history records only a few exceptions: Enoch, Elisha, Daniel. Not many others.

A study of the case histories in the Bible proves that although unbroken trust and dependence in God is possible, on-again off-again is probable. For many Christians, the reality has been to experience on-again, off-again surrender. The reality has been that it takes time to learn to depend upon God all of the time, and never upon ourselves. And while God's goal for us is that we always trust Him, we had better admit and recognize the reality that in most cases, we don't reach this goal overnight.

Growth in the Christian life is learning to depend upon God more and more of the time. As we have noticed earlier, dependence upon God is an all-or-nothing proposition. There is no such thing as partial trust or partial surrender. You are either surrendered to God at any given moment, or you are not surrendered to Him and are depending upon yourself.

We abide in Christ day by day through an ongoing relationship with Him. "Do you ask, 'How am I to abide in Christ?' In the same way as you received Him at first. 'As ye have therefore received Christ Jesus the Lord, so walk ye in Him.' 'The just shall live by faith.' "—*Steps to Christ*, p. 69.

As long as we depend upon Him, we will experience all of the victory and obedience that He has to offer.

But at times the enemy may get us to take our eyes off Christ and cease for the moment to depend upon Him. Then we will fall and fail and sin. It happened for many in the Bible; it happens to many today. When that takes place, our part is to turn to Jesus again, claiming again His promise, "If we confess our sins, he is faithful and just to forgive us our sins, and to cleanse us from all unrighteousness." 1 John 1:9. And we continue the relationship with Him. We don't wait two weeks for God to cool off. We don't give up and decide that we'll never make it to the heavenly country. We don't try to "make things right" on our own and *then* come back to Him. We come back to Him immediately, confessing our sin and our need of Him. Through it all, the relationship with God continues.

Growth in the Christian life takes place as we continue to live by faith in Him, as we continue to seek fellowship with Him day by day. For as we come to Christ day by day, He will work in us to bring us to the place of continual dependence upon him.

Thesis 68

You don't grow by trying to grow.

My goal was to be six feet tall. But it wasn't going too well—I had made it only to three feet six! Later, when I had to stand on the front row with the girls for the eighth-grade class picture, it was more than a guy could take! One day it seemed like time to try to help things along.

I went to the kitchen, stood backed up against the door with a ruler across my head, and made a mark. Then I went out into the back yard and hung from the clothesline post for as long as I could stand it. Then I rushed back in to the door and measured again. What a disappointment! It hadn't helped a bit!

Jesus said, "Which of you by taking thought can add one cubit unto his stature?" Matthew 6:27. You don't grow by trying to grow. In fact, the more you work on trying to grow, the less you grow. If I had spent all my time hanging from the clothesline post, not only would I have never become six feet tall, but it wouldn't have been too long until I would have been six feet under!

Ellen White wrote to our church a long time ago, "The plants and flowers grow not by their own care or anxiety or effort, but by receiving that which God has furnished to minister to their life. The child cannot, by any anxiety or power of its own, add to its stature. No more can you, by anxiety or effort of yourself, secure spiritual growth."—*Steps to Christ*, p. 68.

Even small children understand the principle of growth. You can ask them, "Which would you rather work on, growing or eating?"

It doesn't take them long to figure it out. If they work on growing, they will accomplish neither. If they work on eating, they will accomplish both.

Are you interested in growing spiritually? You cannot grow by focusing on growth. Probably nothing is more detrimental to spiritual growth than to be constantly checking yourself for fruit. The way to grow is by eating—by partaking of the Bread of Life and the Water of Life. The one who experiences the most rapid growth is the one who looks away from self and concentrates on the Sun of Righteousness. The one who is dwarfed is the one who spends the most time trying to grow.

Many people have had the idea that spiritual birth comes from God but that spiritual life is their own responsibility. "Many have an idea that they must do some part of the work alone. They have trusted in Christ for the forgiveness of sin, but now they seek by their own efforts to live aright. But every such effort must fail. Jesus says, 'Without Me ye can do nothing.' Our growth in grace, our joy, our usefulness,—all depend upon our union with Christ. It is by communion with Him, daily, hourly,—by abiding in Him,—that we are to grow in grace. He is not only the Author, but the Finisher of our faith."— *Ibid.*, p. 69.

Is your goal to reach the "measure of the stature of the fulness of Christ"? Ephesians 4:13. You can never reach that goal by hanging from some spiritual clothesline post. It's not possible to grow in grace by our own feeble efforts. Growth is a gift. It is received through association with Christ, through communion with Him. Mankind can never gain for himself that which God has promised to give.

Do you sometimes wonder if you are growing? There's one sure way to tell. Look at whether you are eating! The eating determines the growing every time.

Thesis 69

Christians grow stronger by realizing their weakness. When they are weak, then they are strong.

Bill had been in the same fix so many times he had lost count. So had the doctor, who now stood shaking his head, looking down at Bill's unshaven face and bloodshot eyes.

"I guess I'm hopeless, aren't I, doctor?" Bill said.

"Yes, I guess you are."

"Then how about giving me one more drink, since it won't make any difference anyway.

"OK, I'll give you a drink," the doctor replied surprisingly. "But first you have to do a favor for me."

"What's that?" asked Bill.

"Down the hall," replied the doctor, "is a young man who is in here for the first time. I've given up on you—but he might be able to change. I want you to go down to his room and just let him get a look at you—that's all. Maybe if he sees you it will scare him enough to keep him from having to be brought in here again."

Bill agreed, and went down the hall to find the young man who, like himself, had been brought to the hospital to dry out after a drunken spree.

At first he did it just to get one more drink. But Bill began talking to the young man. "Don't waste your life," he urged him. "Look at me. My family is gone, my self-respect is gone. I have no job; I have no friends. I've lost my health and my reputation. Do you want to end up like this?"

"I'll never end up like you," the young man insisted. "I can stop drinking any time I want to."

"That's what I always thought too," Bill replied. "But it's not true. I can't stop. I'm helpless. The only way I'll ever be able to quit is if God Himself gives me the strength. And that's the only way you'll ever be able to stop too. You don't have the power to control your drinking, or you wouldn't be here. You have to learn to depend upon a higher Power."

Bill returned to the hospital many times after that day, but never again as a patient. He never went back to the doctor to collect the promised drink. He returned to talk to others who had been brought in under the same conditions, who were struggling with alcoholism. It was the beginning of Alcoholics Anonymous.

The principles that Bill discovered in his visit with that young man are the basis today of Alcoholics Anonymous. Each person must come to the point of admitting that he has a great need. He is taught to begin by saying, "I *am* an alcoholic." And he is constantly reminded of his dependence upon a higher Power, if the problem is ever to be controlled. In admitting and recognizing weakness he finds strength.

Each of us can make a similar confession: "I *am* a sinner." We must realize as Christians that we don't grow by becoming stronger and stronger. We grow by realizing anew each day how weak we are and how dependent we are upon God's grace. That's what Paul said in 2 Corinthians 12:10: "When I am weak, then am I strong." "When we have a realization of our weakness, we learn to depend upon a power not inherent."— *The Desire of Ages*, p. 493.

This truth can be a threat to strong people. Those who have found security in their own backbone and self-discipline, who are comfortable because of their good behavior, find the thought of admitting weakness offensive. But the one who is strong, or thinks he is strong, feels no need of a Saviour.

Whether we admit it or not, whether we recognize it or not, every one of us is weak. Only as we become aware of our weakness can we be led to seek power outside of and above our own. "Our greatest strength is realized when we feel and acknowledge our weakness."—*Testimonies*, vol. 5, p. 70.

Do you consider yourself a strong person? You can be truly

strong only as you find your strength in Him. Do you considered yourself weak? Then there's good news for you! His strength is made perfect in weakness. See 2 Corinthians 12:9. No matter how strong you think you are, your only real strength comes as you admit your weakness. No matter how weak you are, you can be strong through Him.

Thesis 70

We can do all things through Christ who strengthens us, but without Him we can do nothing.

During a particular college class, we had been studying the "mini-course" in righteousness by faith in Christ alone. We had read the two texts, John 15:5 and Philippians 4:13, that without Him we can do nothing, but with Him we can do all things.

In the process of the discussion, some students were uneasy about John 15:5. One asked, "If we can do nothing without Christ, then doesn't that take away from our worth as human beings? Aren't we created in God's image? Didn't He create us with free choice? It doesn't sound like freedom of choice if we can't accomplish anything without him."

So we made sure to draw the line between *worthless*, and *helpless*. We talked about the fact that while we are helpless to produce righteousness, we are worth everything in the eyes of heaven.

At that point, a young man in the back of the classroom raised his hand. "Why is it then," he asked, "that it's so easy to feel worthless, but so hard to feel helpless?"

Which of the two do you most often feel? Helpless or worthless? The devil has taken every truth and somehow twisted it, hasn't he? God says, "You are worth everything, but you are helpless apart from Me." The devil says "You are worthless. But try hard to change, and maybe somehow, someday, you will be worth something."

One of the most-often expressed fears about the subject of salvation through faith in Christ alone is the fear that it will result in a do-nothing religion. Many people worry about accepting a "passive" faith that results in complete inactivity. We can look at how little we have accomplished in all our years of trying hard to produce righteousness, and we can assume that if we cease to struggle, we would then accomplish nothing at all.

But the reverse is true. Instead of finding that growth stops when we stop trying to grow, we will find that it is only then that true growth can begin. Jesus didn't stop with His statement in John 15:5, that without Him we can do nothing. He also gave us the good news that through Him we can do all things.

The Ministry of Healing puts it this way: "There is no limit to the usefulness of one who, putting self aside, makes room for the working of the Holy Spirit upon his heart and lives a life wholly consecrated to God."—Page 159.

The Bible is filled with the stories of people who lived in complete dependence upon God. Were they passive? They were when it came to relying upon their own strength. But never forget how active passive can be! For the one who acknowledges his own helplessness and accepts the control of God is the one He will use to do great works for Him.

For several years now I have been collecting stories of people in the Bible who did stupid things! Remember Jonathan and his armorbearer taking on the entire Philistine army? What about Joshua going out to conquer Jericho by walking circles around it every day for a week? Or commanding the sun to stand still when he needed a few more hours to finish a particular battle? It wasn't smart military strategy for Gideon to send home 99 percent of his army and then to attack with pitchers and torches. Elijah was foolish to pour barrels of water on his sacrifice up there on Mount Carmel, instead of making things as easy for God as possible. And then there was Jehosophat, going to battle at the head of the choir!

If any one of these Bible heroes had been depending upon his own strength, instead of God, he would have been either stupid or suicidal! But when human weakness was united to divine strength, God used these persons to accomplish impossible things for Him.

When God invites us to place complete dependence upon

Him, when He asks us to acknowledge our helplessness apart from Him, He is not opening the door for inactivity. The life controlled by God is the life of highest uselfulness and service. And it is the life that gives evidence of growth and fruitfulness. That life can be yours, if you remember that without Him you can do nothing, but that with Him you can do all things—and get with Him, in personal fellowship and communion.

Thesis 71

Satan has no power to cause those who depend on God to sin, but those who depend on themselves are easily defeated.

You probably have heard the story about the saintly grandmother in the church who never had a bad word to say about anybody. One day, a church member said, almost in frustration, "I'll bet you could find something good to say about the devil himself."

To which she replied, "Well, you certainly have to admire his persistence!"

I might add one to that and say that the devil certainly knows how to tempt people! For centuries it has been his number one study, and he is a master of the art. He knows exactly how our minds work and how to deceive us and trick us and get us to give in to his suggestions. And of course we know that without the Spirit of the Lord to lift up a standard against him, we wouldn't stand a chance.

But when we depend upon God's power, the devil is the one who doesn't stand a chance, and he knows it. "Whosoever abideth in him sinneth not." 1 John 3:6. And *The Great Controversy*, page 530, expands the same thought: "Satan is well aware that the weakest soul who abides in Christ is more than a match for the hosts of darkness, and that, should he reveal himself openly, he would be met and resisted. Therefore he seeks to draw away the soldiers of the cross from their strong fortification."

If Satan knows that even the weakest one who abides in Christ is more than a match for him, then it would be extremely important for us to understand what it means to abide in Christ.

Let's look first at the word *abide*. What does it mean to abide? If you do a study of the word *abide* in Scripture, you will discover that it means simply to stay. So Satan is well aware that the weakest soul who stays in dependence upon Christ is more than a match for the hosts of darkness.

But this brings us to a problem. We have already noticed that it takes time to grow, that the surrender that happened at conversion can often be an on-again, off-again experience while we are learning day by day to know God and to trust Him more perfectly. At times we will look to Him and depend upon His power, and then we experience victory. But at times we look away from Him and try to depend upon our own power, and then we fall and fail and sin.

So it is important to make a difference between the two kinds of abiding that show up in Scripture. We will study this more in the next few Theses, but briefly, there is an abiding daily relationship with Christ, and there is a moment-by-moment abiding dependence upon Him.

Sometimes we get the idea that if we abide, or stay, in a relationship with Him day by day, that we will then experience uninterrupted victory. But it's possible to continue to stay with Christ day by day, through a daily relationship with Him, and yet to *not* stay in dependence upon His power at every given moment. So long as we stay in dependence upon God's power instead of our own, Satan is defeated. But any time we depend upon our own power for strength against temptation, *we* are defeated.

God has no waiting period, no time of probation, no delay in the victory that He has to give. From the first day you come to Him, it is possible to experience all of the overcoming, all of the power over sin, all of the victory and obedience that He has to offer—**so long as** you continue to depend upon His power.

But any time you look away from Christ and try to stand in your own feeble strength, you are sure to fall and fail and sin. It will happen even if you have been in day-by-day relationship with God for 119 years and six months! It happened that way for Moses. He had known God, had spoken to Him as to a friend, face to face. He had led the people of Israel out of the land of

Egypt and almost to the borders of the Land of Promise. But one day he gave in to the devil's attempts to get his attention off Christ, and he tried to handle things in his own power. He lost his temper, took glory to himself that should have belonged to God alone, and ended up striking the rock instead of speaking to it.

If the time comes when you strike the rock, in whatever form it may take in your own life, you can know one thing for sure—somehow, at that moment you have stopped depending upon God's power and have started depending upon yourself. But no matter how weak you are, even if you are the "weakest soul," as you learn to abide in Christ moment by moment, Satan will have no power over you.

Thesis 72

The abiding daily relationship with God leads to abiding surrender, moment-by-moment dependence on Him.

Suppose you are in an elevator, traveling toward the top of the World Trade Center. As the elevator moves steadily upward, you lean over to tie your shoe, slip, and fall down. You have gone down, even while going up!

This is perhaps a feeble illustration of the two different kinds of abiding. We can come to God day by day and abide in Him day by day. It is the abiding daily relationship that gives God control of our direction. If we abide in Him day by day, through a daily relationship with Him, our direction will be upward. We choose whether we will abide in relationship with Him day by day as we choose whether or not to spend that thoughtful hour in contemplation of the life of Christ and in prayer and communion with Him. And so long as we come to Him in an abiding daily relationship, inviting His control of our lives, our direction will be upward.

But many Christians have become painfully aware that even when they have chosen an abiding daily relationship with Christ, at times they still can look away from Him to themselves. And at those times they fall and fail and sin. Which brings us to a second kind of abiding—a moment-by-moment abiding dependence. Even when the abiding daily relationship is unbroken, it is possible for the moment-by-moment abiding dependence to be on-again, off-again.

Let's nail it down to begin with, that it is the abiding daily relationship that determines our direction and our destiny. *Steps to Christ*, pages 57, 58, says: "The character is revealed, not by the occasional good deeds and occasional misdeeds, but by the *tendency* of the habitual words and acts." (Emphasis supplied.)

But the moment-by-moment abiding dependence is what determines victory or defeat in the Christian life. Any time we are looking to Jesus and depending upon His strength, we will experience victory. Any time we look to ourselves and depend upon our own power, we are defeated. Depending upon whether we are strong or weak, defeat may be only inward, or outward as well. If we are strong, we may behave correctly, but fall and fail and sin on the inside. If we are weak, the defeat will be outward as well as inward. But if we are depending upon self instead of upon the power of Jesus, we have no choice but to fall and fail and sin.

If we were going to try to draw a graph of the Christian life, it could look something like this:

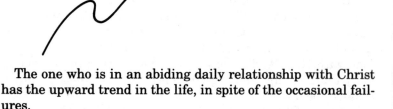

The one who is in an abiding daily relationship with Christ has the upward trend in the life, in spite of the occasional failures.

However, if one is *not* in an abiding daily relationship with Christ, the line would go like this:

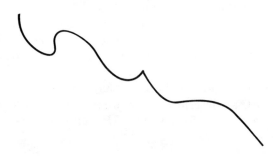

He may have occasional impulses that reach out toward God, but the general trend of the life is downward.

If one is in an abiding daily relationship with Christ, then Christ is in control of his *direction*. If one is not in an abiding daily relationship, the devil has control of his *direction*.

People often ask "Then who is in control at the point of the downward steps, even when the general direction is upward?"

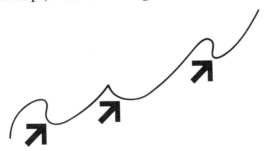

The answer is that the devil is in control, moment-by-moment, any time we look away from Christ and withdraw from dependence upon His power. Of course the devil has to be in control any time we sin. But it's possible for the devil to gain control of our lives for the moment, while God is still in control of our direction. And what makes the difference in God's control of our direction? Again, it's an abiding daily relationship with Him.

God's goal for us is to lead us just as fast as possible to the place where we will know him and trust Him sufficiently so that we will never be turned away from Him, even for the moment. And when that time comes, our lives will look like this:

Thesis 73

Looking to self is always the point of separation from God and breaks the moment-by-moment dependence on Him.

Do you remember when you first began learning to drive a car? You had a lot of things to keep track of, didn't you? You had to check the speedometer and the gas gauge and the rear view mirror and the road ahead, and the directional signs alongside the road and the other cars on the road, and listen to whatever instructions your driving teacher was trying to give you! It's possible to become so involved with all of the mechanics of the process of driving that you forget the most important rule: watch where you are going! When you don't watch where you are going, you don't go where you intended to go.

When I was trying to teach one of my daughters to drive, we went around a corner, and ended up on the lawn of a church. It wasn't exactly the route I had planned for us to take! But we backed up and tried it again, and the day came when she could drive well enough to get her own driver's license. But one thing is certain: it takes more than a driver's license to insure safe driving. If you become preoccupied with the passing scenery, the other cars on the road, or the various items on the dashboard, it doesn't take long to go off the road. If you look at yourself in the rear view mirror and focus your attention there instead of on where you are going, you'll have trouble.

Sometimes when we become Christians, we have the same problems as a new driver. We get involved in the mechanics. We keep looking at ourselves to see how we're doing. We look at other people to see how they're doing. The passing scenery, the pleasures or trials of life here on this earth, divert our attention. And it isn't long until we find ourselves in the ditch, spiritually. It is a law that whenever we take our eyes off Christ and focus on anything else, we lose our way.

Steps to Christ tells us, "When the mind dwells upon self, it is turned away from Christ, the source of strength and life. Hence it is Satan's constant effort to keep the attention diverted from the Saviour and thus prevent the union and communion of the soul with Christ."—Page 71.

Any time the devil succeeds in getting us to look away from Christ, it is inevitable that we fall and fail and sin. Our attention must be on God, and as long as we look to Him we are secure. But when we look to ourselves instead, we have placed ourselves where God should be. And "when man places himself where God should be, he is just where Satan is pleased to have him."—Ellen G. White, *Review and Herald*, January 3, 1899.

Peter discovered this principle in a dramatic way that night on the lake. It's recorded in Matthew 14:28-30. Jesus had fed the 5,000 that day, and heaven had seemed to come down to earth. But just when it looked like the new kingdom could be established on the spot, Jesus sent the disciples away across the lake, more unhappy with Him than they had ever been.

A storm came up, and the disciples feared for their very lives. But Jesus came to them, walking across the water, and Peter said, "Lord, if it be thou, bid me come unto thee on the water. And He said, Come. And when Peter was come down out of the ship, he walked on the water, to go to Jesus. But when he saw the wind boisterous, he was afraid; and beginning to sink, he cried, saying, Lord, save me."

So long as he kept his eyes fixed upon Christ, he was secure. But when he looked instead at the waves and back to the boat to make sure the other disciples were noticing him, he went down.

In the last chapter I talked about the two kinds of abiding, the abiding daily relationship versus the moment-by-moment abiding dependence. When we take our eyes off of Christ, it is the moment-by-moment abiding dependence that is broken— *not* the abiding daily relationship. When we fall and fail and sin, we must come to Christ for repentance and forgiveness.

But our eternal destiny is not decided by the momentary lapse. "If one who daily communes with God [the abiding daily relationship] errs from the path, if he turns a moment from looking steadfastly unto Jesus [the moment-by-moment abiding dependence] it is not because he sins willfully; for when he sees his mistake, he turns again, and fastens his eyes upon Jesus, and the fact that he has erred, does not make him less dear to the heart of God."—Ellen G. White, *Review and Herald,* May 12, 1896.

Thesis 74

God will never separate from us. But we can choose to separate from God.

God never files for divorce! He has given us permission to initiate divorce in the event that our partner has been unfaithful to the marriage vows, but even when His people are unfaithful to Him—even when His people are *repeatedly* unfaithful to Him—He never exercises that right Himself. Breaking off the relationship between God and man is always initiated by mankind, never by God.

God's promise to His people has always been, "I will never leave thee, nor forsake thee." Hebrews 13:5.

In the history of Israel we see almost unlimited opportunity for God to choose to leave His people. They were unfaithful to Him time and time again. They not only broke the commandments spoken from Sinai and written by His own hand, but they became involved in the worship of other gods, forgetting the one true God who had brought them out of Egypt and into the Promised Land. The Old Testament account of their history records over and over again the wickedness and rebellion of kings and people. *The Desire of Ages*, page 28, says, "From the time of their entrance to the land of Canaan, they departed from the commandments of God, and followed the ways of the heathen. It was in vain that God sent them warning by His prophets. In vain they suffered the chastisement of heathen oppression. Every reformation was followed by deeper apostasy."

By the time of Christ, "sin had become a science, and vice was consecrated as a part of religion. Rebellion had struck its roots deep into the heart, and the hostility of man was most violent

16—95 T

against heaven."—*Ibid.*, p. 37. The devil rejoiced that he had done his work so well, that finally God's patience would cease and mankind would be destroyed. But God had a better plan. Instead of destruction, He sent a Saviour. Jesus came to earth to offer reconciliation in person, to try to bridge the gap between mankind and his God.

The offer of mercy that the nation of Israel rejected is still offered to individuals, and every person living on this earth can still accept that offer. Not until every individual has made a final choice for or against God will the offer be withdrawn. When Christ leaves the heavenly sanctuary and probation closes, God's long-suffering will finally come to an end. And even then, God does not arbitrarily leave us; He reluctantly accepts our decision to leave Him. See *The Great Controversy*, p. 614.

Have you ever worried that you are taking too long to learn the lessons He is trying to teach you? Have you ever prayed, "God, please don't give up on me?" You can be assured that He never will. Perhaps a better prayer would be, "God, please help me not to give up on You." For when it comes to the gift of salvation and our relationship with Him, we hold the majority vote. Only our stubborn choice can prevent us from coming into His presence and receiving what He longs to give.

"Who shall separate us from the love of Christ? shall tribulation, or distress, or persecution, or famine, or nakedness, or peril, or sword?" "Nay, in all these things we are more than conquerors through him that loved us. For I am persuaded, that neither death, nor life, nor angels, nor principalities, nor powers, nor things present, nor things to come, nor height, nor depth, nor any other creature, shall be able to separate us from the love of God, which is in Christ Jesus our Lord." Romans 8:35, 37-39.

Thesis 75

The reason God wants us to witness is primarily for our good.

Suppose that one day I begin walking from San Francisco to Pacific Union College—the Promised Land! You come along in your car and stop and offer me a ride. If I get in and ride with you, I will get to PUC quicker; I will be saved a lot of blisters. But I was headed there anyway.

Let's reverse it. One day I begin walking from San Francisco to Reno—the other place! You come along in your car, and stop, and offer me a ride. If a get in and ride with you, I will get to Reno quicker; I will be saved a lot of blisters along the way (although I'll get a lot more blisters when I get there!). But I would have gotten to Reno anyway.

This is an attempt at a parable on the subject of witnessing—and our part in going and telling and sharing the gospel. Sometimes theologians argue about *special* revelation versus *general* revelation. Those in favor of special revelation say that in order for someone to be saved, he has to hear the story of Christ and accept it specifically. The special revelationist insists that unless those who have already come to Christ will go and tell and share, people will be lost eternally.

On the other hand, the general revelationist believes that God will judge each individual on the basis of the light he has received, and that if the most a person knew in his lifetime was to respond to God in nature, that will be enough.

You can look at it from a philosophical standpoint and conclude that since God is a God of love, and since God is fair and just, He could not cause someone else to be lost on the basis of what I do or don't do. There is some pretty good support for this position from inspired sources as well. John 1:9 says that Christ is the Light, "which lighteth every man that cometh into the world." A comment in the *Review and Herald*, June 22, 1911, reads, "In the day of judgment, when the question comes to you as to why you did not obey the commandments of God, you can not make an acceptable excuse on the plea of another's disobedience."

Without question, we can bring the good news of salvation to others and be used as God's instruments to reach them for Him. As in the parable about walking to the Promised Land, we can cut short their search for God, perhaps by years, if we go and tell and share. But God does not leave it with us to determine their eternal destiny.

If this is true, then what is the purpose of the Christian witness? We have often heard appeals to help spread the gospel for the sake of those "out there." But if God can reach them without our help, why does He ask us to become involved. Wouldn't it have been better to leave the work of soul-winning to the angels, who surely are more capable than we will ever be? We are told that in the end, angels will do the work men might have done. See *Selected Messages*, bk. 1, p. 118. If that is going to happen at the end, then why not now, and save all of the mistakes we make in our attempts to share our faith.

The answer is found in understanding God's purpose in giving us a part to act in Christian witness. If you want the best summary of Christian witness, read one chapter in *Steps to Christ*, "The Work and the Life." "The effort to bless others will react in blessings upon ourselves. This was the purpose of God in giving us a part to act in the plan of redemption."—Page 79. *Testimonies*, volume 3, page 391, states it even more clearly: "Whatever necessity there is for our agency in the advancement of the cause of God, He has purposely arranged for our good."

Sometimes people are afraid that if we accept this truth, it will destroy all motivation for going and telling and sharing! It seems self-centered to become involved in service for our own sake, rather than for the sake of others. But please notice that there is a difference between *God's* purpose in involving us in the Christian witness and *our* purpose in becoming involved. We become active in service for Him because we have something to tell and can't wait to share it. We become involved in service because we want others to understand the truth that has set us free. We reach out to others because we have been honored with the privilege of being workers together with God.

As we reach out, for the sake of others and for the sake of God Himself, the inevitable result is that our own souls are blessed. And from God's perspective, that's what He had in mind all along!

Thesis 76

The desire to share comes naturally for the genuine Christian (although methods may very).

You cannot keep your parakeet sealed up in Tupperware! I'm not saying you *should* not; I'm saying you *cannot*. If you attempt such a thing, you won't have a parakeet any longer. You will have a pathetic little heap of feathers!

Steps to Christ, page 78, says, "No sooner does one come to Christ than there is born in his heart a desire to make known to others what a precious friend he has found in Jesus; the saving and sanctifying truth cannot be shut up in his heart. If we are clothed with the righteousness of Christ and are filled with the joy of His indwelling Spirit, we shall not be able to hold our peace. If we have tasted and seen that the Lord is good we shall have something to tell."

You can find similar statements all through the spirit of prophecy. "Jesus did not bid the disciples, 'Strive to *make* your light shine;' He said, '*Let* it shine.' If Christ is dwelling in the heart, it is impossible to conceal the light of His presence." *Thoughts from the Mount of Blessing*, p. 41. "The very first impulse of the renewed heart is to bring others also to the Saviour."—*The Great Controversy*, p. 70.

The desire to share the good news with others comes naturally to the genuine Christian. The desire to share good news comes naturally to anybody! Perhaps you remember the story of the lepers in the days of the famine in Israel. The city was under siege, and people were starving. A group of lepers decided to venture outside the city, hoping to find a morsel of food. They reasoned that if they were killed in the attempt, that they would have died soon anyway. To their amazement, the enemy had fled in the night, leaving their tents and supplies. The lepers ate and drank and then carried away silver and gold from the first two tents they came to. And then the natural desire to share the good news caught up with them! You can read it in 2 Kings 7:9. "They said one to another, We do not well: this day is a day of good tidings, and we hold our peace." So they went into the city to share what they had discovered.

In spite of the fact that the desire to share comes naturally, it is possible not to share. If you resist the natural desire to share, you lose it—just as you lose your parakeet if you shut it up in Tupperware. "The grace of God will not long abide in the soul of him who, having great privileges and opportunities, remains silent. Such a man will soon find that he has nothing to tell."— Ellen G. White, *Review and Herald*, August 22, 1899.

Which brings us to another important truth: not all of us will share the good news in the same way. All will have a natural desire to share, which all will lose if they refuse to act on it. But not all will use the same method in sharing with others.

The Holy Spirit chooses the gifts of service that He bestows. Not everyone can work by the same method, and not everyone can be reached by the same method. But as Christian witnesses we will each have something personal to share about what Jesus Christ has done for us. One person may have an outgoing personality and feel comfortable stopping strangers on the street to tell them of Christ. Another person may be more retiring and may work best among those with whom he is already acquainted. The *Ministry of Healing*, page 143, says, "Christ's method alone will give true success in reaching the people. The Saviour mingled with men as one who desired their good. He showed His sympathy for them, ministered to their needs, and won their confidence. Then He bade them, 'Follow Me.'"

The "gospel bomb" theory should be exploded! Perhaps you've seen the film "The Gospel Blimp," a satire on some of the witnessing methods used by the immature. People are not saved in masses; they are saved as individuals. And the personal testimony of what Jesus has done for you is still the most convincing argument that you can present.

Thesis 77

The happiest person in the world is the one most involved in serving others. The most miserable person is the one most involved in serving self.

Are you happy? We used to sing a song in Kindergarten, "I'm in-right, out-right, up-right, down-right, happy all the time!" How about being happy all the time? Not too many of us manage that, do we? Even Pollyanna found a time when her endless good cheer ended!

But one thing is for sure: whatever happiness you have found in your life has come as a result of forgetting yourself and reaching out to help others. The person who is the most involved in serving self is always the most miserable.

"It is in a life of service only that true happiness is found. He who lives a useless, selfish life is miserable."—*In Heavenly Places*, p. 229. "Those who labor hardest to secure their own happiness are miserable. Those who forget self in their interest for others have reflected back upon their own hearts the light and blessing they dispense to them."—*Ibid.*, p. 325.

One of God's goals for His people is that they are happy. Sometimes religionists have overlooked that fact and thought that the one who wears the dark clothes and the solemn expression is the one who is closest to God. But that is not the case. While it is true that there is more to happiness than the froth and glitter portrayed by the advertising people, it is also true that Christians are to be the happiest people in the world.

The story is told of a sober and somber "Christian" who tried to share his faith. And his friend replied, "I don't think I want to become a Christian. You seem to me to be like a man with a headache. You don't want to get rid of your head, but it pains you to keep it!"

What is it about our human reasoning that causes us to think that the times when we are closest to God are the times when we have to be the most solemn? Have you ever looked around you during the Communion Service at church? It's a service intended and designed to be a celebration of sins forgiven and the assurance of peace with God. But don't you dare smile! If you do, you'll be the only one!

Sometimes I have tried to convince people that it's not a sin to smile during the Lord's Supper—but I've never been very successful. As the deacons pass the emblems up and down the aisles, the atmosphere is very close to that of a funeral. Some of us are tempted to smile at the sober faces around us, but we quickly get the victory!

The Communion Service is to be a joyous experience! The worship of God is to be a joyous experience! The service of God is to be a joyous experience. Christians should be the happiest people in the world—and one major reason that can be true is that the genuine Christian is always thinking of others, reaching out to others, and thus losing sight of self.

And this reaching out to others inevitably brings blessing upon the one who does the reaching out. "Whosoever will save his life shall lose it; but whosoever shall lose his life for my sake and the gospel's, the same shall save it." Mark 8:35. To give is to gain. "Those who minister to others will be ministered unto by the Chief Shepherd. They themselves will drink of the living water, and will be satisfied. They will not be longing for exciting amusements, or for some change in their lives. The great topic of interest will be, how to save the souls that are ready to perish."—*The Desire of Ages,* p. 641.

Are you happy? Or are you miserable? Your involvement in blessing others makes the difference.

Thesis 78

Christian service in the spiritual life corresponds to exercise in the physical life.

When Captain Eddie Rickenbacker's plane went down in the Pacific during World War II, the survivors floated in a life raft without food or water for several weeks before finally being rescued. Rickenbacker and his lieutenant, James Whittaker, wrote about their experience in the book *We Thought We Heard the Angels Sing*. One of their crew members died during the ordeal, and the rest spent quite awhile debating whether or not to eat his body, before they finally buried him at sea.

But suppose that just before these men were rescued, I happened to come along in my speedboat. The men in the raft stare up at me through sunken eyes, wondering if I'm just another mirage. But I pull up beside them and say, "You guys have a problem. You don't look too healthy. What you need is more exercise!"

And they reply, "What *you* need is more brains!"

For a long time I had the idea that the way to get people interested in spiritual things was to get them involved in witness and service and outreach. In a new parish, I would therefore enlist the help of the super-salesmen among the membership and try to get everybody out knocking on doors or passing out literature or giving Bible studies.

About 5 percent of the people responded and did indeed try to witness. But it was really a loss. In fact, it caused many to pull away in order to avoid feeling guilty for not becoming involved.

It's foolish to try to get people to exercise if they are nearly dead. It's foolish, and indeed futile, to try to get people to exer-

251

cise if they haven't even been born yet.

So then I decided to try another technique. When going to a new church, I would do everything possible to get people interested in spiritual things. I would begin by emphasizing our relationship with God and the things that have to do with faith and surrender and overcoming. The response was overwhelming—at first. But then it peaked and died away. And I moved on to another congregation!

Finally I realized the problem. It's vital to begin with an emphasis upon spiritual things—but that must be followed as quickly as possible by encouraging the people to become active in Christian service. We can keep new life in Christ alive only as we share it. And the only thing that will keep revival from fading away is to begin at once to share the good news with others.

This balance is described in the book *Steps to Christ*, pages 80, 81: "Strength comes by exercise; activity is the very condition of life. Those who endeavor to maintain Christian life by passively accepting the blessings that come through the means of grace, and doing nothing for Christ, are simply trying to live by eating without working. And in the spiritual as in the natural world, this always results in degeneration and decay. A man who would refuse to exercise his limbs would soon lose all power to use them. Thus the Christian who will not exercise his God-given powers not only fails to grow up into Christ, but he loses the strength that he already had."

Christ used the best method in working with His disciples. First, He called them to follow him. See Matthew 4:19. Then after a time, He gave them the commission, "Go ye therefore, and teach all nations, baptizing them in the name of the Father, and of the Son, and of the Holy Ghost." Matthew 28:19.

Only as we learn how to follow Him—and to keep on following Him—are we prepared to go.

Thesis 79

We cannot give to others that which we do not ourselves possess.

Imagine with me a courtroom scene. The witness is sworn in, agreeing to tell "the truth, the whole truth, and nothing but the truth." He takes his seat in the witness stand, and the questioning begins.

"Where were you on the night of the crime?"

"At home."

"What were you doing?"

"I was in bed asleep."

"Did you see anything unusual?"

"No."

"Hear anything?"

"No, I slept right through the whole thing."

"And you're a *witness*?"

At this point the "witness" is sent out of the courtroom, right?

There's an interesting story in the Old Testament about a witness who had nothing to tell. Absalom had been working to take over the kingdom of his father David. There had been a battle, and in the heat of the battle Absalom's mule went under a low-hanging branch, and Absalom was hanged by his hair! A man named Cushi was a witness and was instructed to go tell King David what he had seen.

But another man also wanted to run. His name was Ahimaaz. He went to the officer in charge and said, "Let me run too."

The officer replied, "Why do you want to run? You haven't any news to report."

But Ahimaaz insisted. And ran well, in spite of his lack of information! In fact, he ran so well that he overtook the real witness, Cushi, and arrived before he did. He fell on his face before the king and said, "All is well"—which it wasn't. But when David pressed him for details concerning Absalom, all he could reply was, "I saw a great tumult, but I knew not what it was." 2 Samuel 18:29.

Many people within the Christian faith have run with Ahimaaz! Their zeal has been great, but their message is feeble. In order to be an effective witness, you have to have something to witness to! "Without a living faith in Christ as a personal Saviour it is impossible to make our influence felt in a skeptical world. We cannot give to others that which we do not ourselves possess. It is in proportion to our own devotion and consecration to Christ that we exert an influence for the blessing and uplifting of mankind. If there is no actual service, no genuine love, no reality of experience, there is no power to help."—*Thoughts From the Mount of Blessing*, p. 37.

The first step in becoming a witness for Christ is to have an experience with Him for yourself. It's not enough to have seen a change in the lives of others, or to have sensed the power and excitement of the gospel. The Christian witness must always be based on the first-person. No one is going to be impressed by a witness to Christianity who can only say, "I saw a great tumult, but I knew not what it was."

The witness for which the world is waiting today is the testimony that Jesus commissioned the restored demoniacs of Gadara to present. He said, "Go home to thy friends, and tell them how great things the Lord hath done for thee, and hath had compassion on thee." Mark 5:19.

Thesis 80

The real issue in temptation is whether to live life apart from Christ.

Have you ever been tempted? Have you ever found yourself struggling with temptation? I might add another question: Are you a human being? Temptation is a fact of life on this earth, isn't it? And many of us have discovered by personal experience that there is a devil, long before we discover by personal experience that there is a God.

As a teenager, I concluded that my problems with temptation should be over and done with by the time I reached my twenties. But when I was in my twenties, I decided it was going to take a few more years. I would experience freedom from temptation in my thirties, I decided. But each new decade brought its own set of problems. I hate to admit what age I'm aiming for now! The painful reality is that we live in a world of temptation, that the devil is alive and well, and that he never leaves anyone completely alone. His persistence is equaled only by his malice, and when he can't cause someone to sin, he is willing to settle for causing them to suffer. Temptation is not a pleasant experience! Hebrews 2:18 says of Christ, "For in that he himself hath suffered being tempted, he is able to succour them that are tempted."

But when temptation ends in failure and defeat and sin, the suffering is even worse. If we could only discover how to handle temptation, we would be in a position to answer a major question that many people are asking. Often the methods proposed for handling temptation depend upon how much willpower a person has or does not have, and what appears to work for the strong is ineffective for the weak.

As we begin to consider this subject, let's remember again that sin is not based upon behavior. We've already studied the fact that *sin,* singular, is living life apart from Christ, and that sin*s*, plural, (doing wrong things) are the result of that separation.

In the same way, we can draw a distinction between *temptation,* singular (the temptation to live life apart from a day-by-day relationship with Christ) and temptation*s*, plural, which would have to do with wrong actions, or wrong behavior.

If I am struggling with temptation*s*, plural, then what is my real problem? It is the lack of a constant trust in God. That's why the devil does everything he can to separate us from an ongoing relationship with Christ, for that is where our trust in God develops. If the devil can get us to choose to live life independently of Jesus Christ, temptation*s* plural, will be successful as a matter of course.

"The soul that loves God, loves to draw strength from Him by constant communion with Him. When it becomes the habit of the soul to converse with God, the power of the evil one is broken; for Satan cannot abide near the soul that draws nigh unto God."—Ellen G. White Comments, *S.D.A. Bible Commentary*, vol. 7, p. 937.

So let's nail it down right to begin with, that the real issue in temptation is to live life apart from Christ. If you are giving in to the temptation to begin each day without taking time for prayer and the study of God's Word, if you are living life at a distance from the Lord Jesus, then you have lost the battle already. Temptation*s* can be overcome only from within the framework of a relationship with Christ. And as we go on to consider how to handle temptation*s*, plural, it must always be from the base of having first understood how to handle *temptation,* singular—the temptation to live separated from God.

But the Christian who is daily surrendering to Christ and spending time learning to know Him better and trust Him more may still find that not only is he tempted, but that he has given in to temptation*s*. If that is true for you, then a study of the mechanics of temptation*s* may bring a breakthrough.

Thesis 81

Temptations become sins when we consent to them in our minds.

Let's suppose that when you got up this morning you chose to spend a thoughtful hour in prayer and in contemplation of the life of Christ. You invited Him to take control of your life and accepted His gifts of repentance and forgiveness for the new day. You laid your plans at His feet, inviting Him to direct your ways. And then you went about your work.

But before evening, you found that you had sinned. You had given in to one of the devil's temptations, and as you looked back on what happened, you found yourself asking, "Why? How? When did I go wrong?"

Consider, for a few moments, the "anatomy" of a temptation.

We have already studied the fact that as long as your eyes remain fixed upon Christ, sin has no power over you. When you began your day with God, you placed yourself under His control. As long as you continue in dependence upon Him, the devil has no power to cause you to sin. In fact, when you are depending upon Christ, sins will be hateful to you. Therefore the devil knows better than to waste his time trying to tempt you to do wrong things. First, he must somehow divert your attention from Jesus and dependence upon Him. *Thoughts from the Mount of Blessing*, page 92, says, "Yielding to temptation begins in permitting the mind to waver, to be inconstant in your trust in God."

We have already noticed the devil's tactics to get your eyes off Jesus. (See the list in *Steps to Christ*, page 71.) He causes you to become absorbed in pleasures, in cares, perplexities and sorrows, in the faults of others, in your own faults and imperfections, or in anxiety over whether you shall be saved. As you turn away from Christ and begin to depend upon yourself, your defense has departed from you and the devil can then come in with his temptations to do wrong things, which you will inevitably find appealing.

This transfer of the attention from Christ to self, this change from an abiding dependence in God to self-dependence, often happens imperceptibly. Your first clue that anything has changed may come when you're presented with one of the enemy's temptations and find it attractive.

Edward Vick, in his book *Let Me Assure You*, gives five steps in temptations: temptation, consider, consent, plan, act. Let's look at each step.

1. *Temptation:* The devil presents his enticement to commit sins. He cannot compel us; he can only invite. It's no sin to be tempted. Jesus was.

2. *Consider:* God does not bypass our minds. We do not obtain victory apart from our own intelligence. Even Christ considered the temptation the devil presented to Him long enough to see the issues involved. Considering what is at stake and recognizing the temptation for what it is does not involve sin.

If you are depending upon Jesus at the time of temptations, you will stop right here. The Spirit of the Lord will lift up a standard against the enemy, and you will be given the victory. But if you have turned your attention away from Jesus to self and are depending upon your own strength, you have no choice but to proceed to the next step, which is where temptations become sins—the point of consent.

3. *Consent:* What is consent? It is the response that says, "Hey! that sounds like fun!" It doesn't necessarily have to be "Yes, I'll *do* it." For sins begin before actions begin. Jesus said in Matthew 5 that if you are angry, you are guilty of murder, and if you lust, you are guilty of adultery. It's not necessary to go any farther than Step 3 to be guilty before God of sin. "The prevalence of a sinful *desire* shows the delusion of the soul." *Thoughts From the Mount of Blessing*, p. 92.

4. *Plan:* Depending upon the nature of the temptation, this

step may be brief or fairly complicated. Sometimes even the strong-willed person, who by sheer grit and determination can keep from going on to step 5, will still spend time here because it can be fun to make plans! The weak will plan, and then go ahead with those plans.

5. *Act:* Finally, the plan becomes action, at least for the weak. But notice that this is *not* the step that determines whether a person has sinned. Sin began back at step 3, when the consent was given.

The good news is that at any point along the way in these five steps, you can recognize your danger and turn to Christ for repentance and forgiveness. He is always willing to accept us, no matter when we come to Him. As long as we continue to seek a relationship and fellowship with Him day by day, He will bring us to the point where we will depend upon Him all of the time, not just part of the time. When that time comes, the enemy will bring his temptations to us in vain.

Thesis 82

Jesus was tempted to do right, but in His own power, and so are we.

Have you ever been tempted to turn stones into bread? I've struggled with a lot of temptations, but never that one! Why? Because the devil knows he would be wasting his time. I couldn't do it even if I wanted to.

Is there anything wrong with turning stones into bread? Is there anything wrong with being hungry when you haven't eaten for six weeks? Jesus, later in His ministry, and under His Father's direction, multiplied the loaves and fishes by supernatural power and fed them to people who had been fasting only since breakfast! The devil didn't tempt Christ to turn the stones into fudge brownies or Baskin Robbins ice cream. He tempted Him to turn stones into bread—and that sounds like a pretty good thing to do when you have eaten nothing for forty days and nights.

All the temptations that the devil came up with to turn Jesus from His mission had one common denominator. Every one was designed to get Jesus to stop depending upon His Father's power and use the power with which He was born.

Sins were repulsive to Jesus. Hebrews 1:8, 9 says it in so many words, He "loved righteousness, and hated iniquity." So the devil would have been unable to attract Him by temptations to do wrong things. His only possibility was to try to get Him to do what was right—but in His own power.

We will look at the nature of Christ in more detail in theses 90 through 94. But to understand the subject of temptation, we need at least this much: Jesus was not tempted to do wrong things. He was tempted to do right things, but to do them in His own power—and we are tempted with the same thing.

Revelation 3:14-22 records the message to the Laodicean church. Laodicea isn't short on works, but a relationship with Jesus is missing. Jesus is pictured as on the outside, knocking for admission. The Laodicean needs to repent for his sin—not his sins. He has been living his spotless life apart from Christ. He has forgotten that "with God outward show weighs nothing. The outward forms of religion, without the love of God in the soul, are utterly worthless."—Ellen G. White Comments, *S.D.A. Bible Commentary*, vol. 7, p. 958. Laodicea is a church filled with strong people who feel no need of a Saviour.

But there's good news for Laodicea, in verse 21—a promise to the one who overcomes. And the method for overcoming? We can overcome in the same way Christ overcame. As Christ depended upon power from above Him, instead of power from within Him, so can we.

The devil will try to overcome us in the same way he tried to overcome Christ. And, as we are painfully aware, he is often successful in diverting our attention from the Saviour. He doesn't come to us and ask if we would be interested in committing some heinous sin. He just tries to fill our days and hours and minutes with a multitude of things, good in themselves, that take our attention away from Jesus. He tries to keep us too busy to spend time in fellowship and relationship with Christ. He doesn't even care if we're busy working for the church, just as long as we're too busy for Jesus Christ. That's the bottom line. He doesn't worry about the "good" things we do, as long as we do them in our own strength.

But we have been warned of the danger. Jesus not only came to die for us, He came to show us how to live. He came to show us how to resist the enemy's temptation to pull away from our relationship with God and depend upon ourselves. When we understand the issues involved in sin and temptation, we will know where our strength lies. As we refuse to separate ourselves from dependence upon Christ, even for "good" reasons, we will be overcomers through the power of God.

Thesis 83

The Lord knows how to deliver the godly out of temptations, but not the ungodly.

For a number of years now I have pastored college churches. Teaching one class at the college each semester has helped me to keep in touch with the student population. And it continues to remind me of the foolishness of the grading system! Students learn early to play games as an escape from studying the very subjects they supposedly came to study! They try to analyze the teacher and his techniques. They coast along most of the semester and then try to cram just enough at the last minute to make it through with a passing grade.

My students try to outwit my attempts to teach them something, so I have begun to try to outwit them! In the process I've come up with "contract grading." I guarantee every student who will attend class regularly and faithfully do the homework day by day a passing grade—no matter how poorly he may do on the tests and quizzes.

The amazing thing (and the amusing thing) is that after years of teaching and hundreds of students, not once has a student who attended class regularly and handed in the daily work, failed to make a passing grade anyway. By the time he sits through the lectures and does the homework, he has no trouble passing the tests and quizzes!

But my promise still stands. Those who do faithful work day by day will be delivered at exam time!

God has promised to deliver the godly from temptation. You can read it in 2 Peter 2:9. "The Lord knoweth how to deliver the godly out of temptations."

But who are the "godly"? Have you ever had the idea that if you were "godly," you wouldn't need any help handling temptation? Psalm 1:6 says, "The Lord knoweth the way of the righteous: but the way of the ungodly shall perish." So the godly are the righteous—and the ungodly are the unrighteous. Those who are godly, or righteous, are the ones who are not depending on themselves, or their own righteousness, but on the righteousness of Christ. These are the ones the Lord knows how to deliver out of temptation. Those who are ungodly, or unrighteous, are the ones who depend upon their own righteousness and their own power. But they have none! Even God is unable to deliver from temptation those who insist on trusting in themselves.

Would it be safe to say that the Lord is *not* able to deliver the ungodly out of temptation? How often have you been defeated in your attempts to live the Christian life because, in a crisis, you try to draw on reserve power that you don't have? It's like trying to pass an examination for which you've made no preparation. Or writing a check when you have no money in the bank to cover it.

The Ministry of Healing, page 510, tells us that "when we permit our communion with God to be broken, our defense is departed from us. Not all your good purposes and good intention will enable you to withstand evil. You must be men and women of prayer."

As you seek the Lord day by day and are changed by beholding Him, you learn the futility of depending upon your own feeble strength. When you stop trying to fight sin and the devil yourself, then the Lord is finally able to bring deliverance. He has all power in heaven and in earth, and when you rely upon His power, victory is assured.

Thesis 84

Temptations are not overcome at the time of temptation, but always before.

One time I heard a preacher in the pulpit give several examples of how he thought we should overcome temptation. "Suppose you have a problem with alcohol," he said. "You go down to the liquor store and purchase a bottle of wine. You get back in your car, remove the cover of the bottle, and lift it to your lips. Suddenly, you are aware that you are being tempted!"

Well, I guess so!

But he continued. "Suppose you have a problem with drugs, and you contact your drug dealer and purchase a supply of the strongest stuff. You return to your apartment, get out your syringe, heat up the mixture, and just as you are ready to plunge the needle into your arm, you realize that you are being tempted. What do you do?"

Perhaps one of our biggest problems with temptation has been that we wait until the times described by this preacher and *then* try to decide what to do. But by then it's too late! If sin begins in the mind, in allowing our trust and dependence in Christ to be broken, then the temptation was presented and given in to long before. If sins are not just wrong actions, but wrong thoughts and plans and desires as well (as we have noticed in the last few chapters), then the temptation was successful even before the trip to the liquor store or the drug dealer. The temptation had already become sin at the point of consenting in the mind. Planning and acting out the sin followed, and were simply the inevitable results of the sin that had already taken place.

Thoughts From the Mount of Blessing, page 60, tells us: "The season of temptation, under which, it may be, one falls into grievous sin, does not create the evil that is revealed, but only develops or makes manifest that which was hidden and latent in the heart. As a man 'thinketh in his heart, so is he:' for out of the heart 'are the issues of life.' Proverbs 23:7; 4:23."

If you find yourself flunking an examination in calculus, the real problem took place when you failed to learn your multiplication tables or neglected to solve the daily assignments. If you find yourself unexpectedly overdrawn at the bank, the real problem took place when you didn't write down the checks you sent out or didn't add or subtract correctly. If you find yourself drowning in the deep end of the swimming pool, the real problem is that you haven't learned how to stay afloat in the shallow end first.

The strong have used all sorts of techniques to try to overcome sin at the time of the temptation. The weak try the same techniques and find that they make no difference in the outcome. The problem is not finding the right words to say or prayer to pray or song to sing at the time of the temptation. The problem is finding the Source of power, so that when the temptation comes the Spirit of the Lord lifts up a standard against the enemy in your behalf.

Any method that tries to force right behavior at the actual moment of temptation is going to focus your attention on yourself, and that is a dead-end street right there. The only way anyone ever overcomes sin and the devil is through looking to Jesus—not to self. Even the strong have discovered that when they are separated from Christ, all they can hope to control is the outward action. They cannot change the desire of their hearts.

When Jesus came to His disciples in the Garden and found them sleeping, He said to them, "Rise and pray, lest ye enter into temptation." Luke 22:46. Were they being tempted at that time? Well, they were being tempted to sleep. But the thing that set them up for defeat when temptations came, was the fact that they gave in to the temptation to neglect available power from above. And because of their neglect, when the crisis came, they all forsook Him and fled.

Hebrews 4:16 tells us to "come boldly unto the throne of grace, that we may obtain mercy, and find grace to help in time of need." Too often we have read instead that we are to come boldly to the throne of grace in time of need. It's true that Jesus always accepts us whenever we turn to Him, but only by seeking His mercy at the throne of grace *now* will we have grace to help when the time of need comes. He always offers forgiveness from sin—but if we are delivered from sinning, it will be because we have come to Him for His power before the season of temptation ever arrives. We gain the victory by learning to abide in Him day by day, and moment by moment.

Thesis 85

Victory is not something we achieve. It is something we receive.

One theme runs throughout all of the messages to the seven churches in Revelation 1-3. Overcoming. A special promise is given to each church, a promise to those who are overcomers. To the church of Ephesus: "To him that overcometh will I give to eat of the tree of life, which is in the midst of the paradise of God." Revelation 2:7. To the church in Smyrna: "He that overcometh shall not be hurt of the second death." Verse 11. To the church in Pergamos: "To him that overcometh will I give to eat of the hidden manna, and will give him a white stone, and in the stone a new name written, which no man knoweth saving he that receiveth it." Verse 17.

Thyatira: "He that overcometh, and keepeth my works unto the end, to him will I give power over the nations." Verse 26. To the church of Sardis: "He that overcometh, the same shall be clothed in white raiment; and I will not blot out his name out of the book of life, but I will confess his name before my Father, and before his angels." Revelation 3:5.

To the church of Philadelphia: "Him that overcometh will I make a pillar in the temple of my God, and he shall go no more out: and I will write upon him the name of my God, and the name of the city of my God, which is new Jerusalem, which cometh down out of heaven from my God: and I will write upon him my new name." Verse 12.

And finally, to the church of Laodicea: "To him that overcometh will I grant to sit with me in my throne, even as I also overcame, and am set down with my Father in his throne." Verse 21.

Sounds as though being an overcomer is pretty important, doesn't it? The Lord certainly gives the one who overcomes some mighty incentives to do so: to be able to eat of the tree of life, of the hidden manna, to receive a new name, to have power over the nations, to be clothed in white raiment, to be a pillar in God's temple, and to sit down with Christ in His throne.

Sometimes people get the idea when I say that victory is a gift, that it is somehow not that important. Nothing could be further from the truth. Salvation is a gift—is salvation important? Faith is a gift—is faith important? Repentance is a gift—is repentance important? God's goal for us is victory—and even more than victory. He wants us to be "more than conquerors" through Him. Romans 8:37.

When God talks about getting the victory, and even "more" than the victory, what victory is it that He is describing? Is it the victory over sins? No. It's a victory over something far more difficult to control. *Thoughts From the Mount of Blessing*, page 141: "The Christian life is a battle and a march. But the victory to be gained is not won by human power. The field of conflict is in the domain of the heart. The battle which we have to fight—the greatest battle that was ever fought by man—is the surrender of self to the will of God, the yielding of the heart to the sovereignty of love."

Notice it is the surrender of *self*, giving up on ourselves and giving God control, that is the issue—not the surrender of wrong things.

It's perhaps the only battle in the universe in which the way to victory lies in giving up! And since that is true, then it is inevitable that victory would have to be a gift, for surrender is a gift. "We cannot, of ourselves, conquer the evil desires and habits that strive for the mastery. We cannot overcome the mighty foe who holds us in his thrall. God alone can give us the victory."—*Ibid.*, p. 142.

We already noticed the method for obtaining the victory that God gives in the message to the church of Laodicea. "To him that overcometh will I grant to sit with me in my throne, *even as I also overcame*, and am set down with my Father in his throne." (Emphasis supplied.) How did Jesus overcome?

Through dependence upon His Father's power and through relationship with His Father—not through fighting the devil in His own strength, even though He had the strength, which we do not. Through trust in His Father's power and might, Jesus was Victor. And through trusting in Him, through faith in Him, we too will gain the victory. "This is the victory that overcometh the world, even our faith." 1 John 5:4.

Thesis 86

In the Christian warfare we are active toward the fight of faith and passive toward the fight of sins.

All sorts of exercise programs flood the market today. Exercise has become so popular that some people have seriously damaged their health overdoing it. But I have an exercise that I would like you to try for your spiritual health. An exercise that will make you strong to gain the victory! Are you ready? I want you to stand still and go forward at the same time!

The Lord assigned this particular exercise to the Israelites right at the beginning of their trip to the Promised Land. You can read about it in Exodus 14:13-15. They were at the banks of the Red Sea, closed in by mountains on either side, and the enemy was coming rapidly from behind. Just when they were about to panic completely, the Lord sent a message through Moses. "Fear ye not, stand still, and see the salvation of the Lord, which he will shew to you to day: for the Egyptians whom ye have seen to day, ye shall see them again no more for ever. The Lord shall fight for you, and ye shall hold your peace. And the Lord said unto Moses, Wherefore criest thou unto me? speak unto the children of Israel, that they go forward."

There you have it, a Bible endorsed exercise program! Stand still and go forward. That's all there is to it.

Is it possible to stand still and go forward at the same time? Well, you have probably done it before! Have you ever stood on a bus or train or airplane, while it was going forward? Did you stand still? Most people realize the futility of jogging up and down the aisles of a bus or plane while it is in motion. Not only is it wasted effort, but you are likely to lose your balance and fall down! So you just stand still. But at the same time, you are going forward—and not only that, but you are going forward at a much greater speed than if you got off the vehicle and tried to run in your own strength.

How were the people of Israel to stand still and go forward at the same time? They were to stand still as far as fighting the enemy was concerned—but they were to go forward in faith! It's the difference between the fight of faith and the fight of sin. God invites us to become involved in the fight of faith. He warns us against becoming involved in the fight of sin.

The fight of faith is the struggle to set aside that thoughtful time each day for prayer and study of the life of Christ, for communication with Him. The fight of sin is the struggle to overcome temptations and sins, to war against the devil and his powers. If we try to fight the fight of sin, we're finished right at the beginning. Ephesians 6:12 tells us that "we wrestle not against flesh and blood, but against principalities, against powers, against the rulers of the darkness of this world, against spiritual wickedness in high places." If we aren't even fighting flesh and blood, then how can *we* fight? How do you fight a spirit? There's only one way. You would have to engage the help of another Spirit to fight your battle for you.

And this is what God has promised to do for us. "Man is not able to save himself, but the Son of God fights his battles for him and places him on vantage ground by giving him his divine attributes."—Ellen G. White, *Review and Herald*, February 8, 1898.

It's true that Paul tells us to put on the whole armor of God—which looks as though there's going to be a fight! But if you examine the armor described in Ephesians 6:11-18, it is armor for a *standing* war. In fact, that's what it says repeatedly. "Put on the whole armor of God, that ye may be able to *stand*." "Having done all, to *stand*." "*Stand* therefore." Notice that every item of the armor of God that we are to put on has to do with a faith relationship with God, or the fight of faith. It is for defense—not armor for attack. The various pieces represent truth, righteousness, the gospel of peace, faith, salvation, prayer, and the Word of God. The person who is thus equipped will be ready to *stand still* in trying to fight the enemy—but to *go forward* in a relationship of faith and trust in God.

Don't try to go forward unless you are standing still—you will be sure to fall! Don't try to stand still without going forward—or you will have only a passive religion that will soon go sour. Stand still *and* go forward. It's the only way to victory!

Thesis 87

Real victory is getting the victory over trying to get the victory.

Jehoshaphat had just received word that the enemy was coming. Instead of calling a council of war and ordering the troups to prepare at once for a major attack, he did a very interesting thing. You can read about it in 2 Chronicles 20. He called a prayer meeting!

At that prayer meeting, one man stood up, led by the Spirit of God, and suggested a plan. He told the people that they were to go out to meet the enemy, but that they would not need to fight, that the Lord would fight for them. So early the next morning they gathered to go out to meet the enemy, and after a short discussion, they decided to send the choir at the head of their company to sing praises to the Lord on the way to the battlefield.

How would you like to have been a member of that choir? It would have been a real victory to get the victory over trying to get the victory, wouldn't it? Can you imagine someone in the bass section sticking a slingshot under his choir robe?

If you had been there that day, it would have taken far more faith to leave the slingshot home and go out in the name of the Lord, singing praises to Him, wouldn't it? But somehow the people managed to do what Jehoshaphat had commanded, and the Lord won a mighty victory for them that day.

In the spiritual life, as well, victory is always won by looking to Jesus and depending upon His power. It is never won by trying to fight sin and the devil. It is never won by trying to "help" God out, allowing Him to do part of the work while we take potshots at the enemy on the side. Victory is God's department. We can cooperate with Him only through seeking a relationship with Him day by day, and thus allowing Him to fight the enemy *for* us.

Perhaps you have tried the school-kid trick of balancing a broom on your hand. If you look at your hand, you're in trouble. But if you concentrate your attention on the broom and look up, suddenly it becomes easy.

When we look to ourselves, we inevitably lose the victory— but when we look to Christ, victory comes as a result. How does the poem go? "I looked at Christ, and the dove of peace flew in. I looked at the dove, and he flew away again."

Most of us have lost the victory, not because we haven't tried hard enough to get the victory, but because we have tried *too hard*. We have been working on the victory itself, and in that very process we lose what we had hoped to gain.

In the growing Christian life, it is possible every day to work to gain the victory—and lose it; or to look to Christ instead of working on victory—and gain it.

Victory is like surrender, for it is based upon surrender. It is all or nothing. There is no such thing as partial victory.

We might illustrate this truth by using a "sin seismograph."

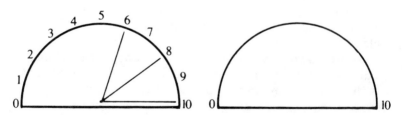

First notice the one on the left. This is the way we have often tried to measure victory. Suppose at the beginning of my Christian life, I have a terrible temper. But I begin trying to get the victory, and after the first few times, my outburst of temper measures only nine on the scale. After several years of being a Christian, losing my temper measures only six. After several more years of earnest effort, the needle only goes to three. And just before I die, I get in one good day, and the needle doesn't even flutter. That is *not* victory!

Instead, notice the illustration on the right. It has only two numbers, zero and ten. Any time I depend upon myself instead of upon Christ, whether I have been a Christian for one day or for a lifetime, the needle will peg itself at ten, every time. Any time I am depending upon Christ instead of myself, whether the first day of my Christian life or the last, the needle won't even flutter.

God's goal for us is that we learn to depend on Him all of the time. It is possible for us, as it was for Christ. *The Desire of Ages*, page 679, says, "He knew that the life of His trusting disciples would be like His, a series of uninterrupted victories, not seen to be such here, but recognized as such in the great hereafter."

What brings the uninterrupted victories? To be a *trusting* disciple. And only as we learn to know Him can we learn to trust Him all of the time. When we trust Him and look to Him, victory is assured.

PERFECTION

Thesis 88

Perfection of character is not our work. It is God's work in us.

Have you ever bought a new car? Remember how it felt when you drove it home for the first time, with its gleaming exterior and spotless upholstery? How did you feel the first time someone dented your fender or one of your children spilled a milkshake in the back seat?

There is a built-in drive for perfection in every human being. We long for perfection, and we are disappointed when something "perfect" is marred. We are unwilling to pay full price for damaged merchandise. We learn even as children that once a thing is broken, the enjoyment is destroyed. Our parents urge us to take care of our things, to put off as long as possible the day when they will wear out and no longer be of value to us.

We work to retain physical perfection. Parents rejoice over the perfection of their newborn child and sorrow over every scar, physical or emotional. We do our best to disguise the evidences of aging in ourselves and sigh over the wrinkles, the sagging skin, the thinning hair, the loss of agility. We long for the time of glorification when the process will be reversed and we will live in perfect bodies.

Perfection is important to every one of us—and it is important to God as well. He has promised us eternal youth, without disease and pain, as we live for eternity in perfect health and beauty. He has told us about our heavenly home, perfect to the last detail—even the flowers there are perfect and will never fade. We are assured of perfect happiness, for He tells us that there will be no more tears or sorrow or crying.

But we don't have to wait until heaven for one kind of perfection. God has also promised perfection of character—and that is to be developed here. God has promised perfection, *commanded* perfection. It is His will for us to be perfect!

God said to Abraham, "Walk before me, and be thou perfect." Genesis 17:1. Jesus told His followers, "Be ye therefore perfect, even as your Father which is in heaven is perfect." Matthew 5:48. Paul wrote, "Let us go on unto perfection." Hebrews 6:1.

Perfection is important; perfection is possible; perfection is necessary for the Christian. But never forget that perfection is *God's* work, not ours. Notice some of the Bible evidence:

"God is my strength and power: and he maketh my way perfect." 2 Samuel 22:33.

"It is God that girdeth me with strength, and maketh my way perfect." Psalm 18:32.

"But the God of all grace, who hath called us unto his eternal glory by Christ Jesus, after that ye have suffered a while, make you perfect, stablish, strengthen, settle you." 1 Peter 5:10.

"Now the God of peace, that brought again from the dead our Lord Jesus, that great shepherd of the sheep, through the blood of the everlasting covenant, make you perfect in every good work to do his will, working in you that which is wellpleasing in His sight, through Jesus Christ; to whom be glory for ever and ever, Amen." Hebrews 13:20, 21.

Are you interested in perfection of character? It is possible for you to have it. It is good news to know that even though our physical bodies decay and our material possessions perish with the using, that our inward life can be renewed day by day. See 2 Corinthians 4:16. Perfect character is available this side of heaven. It is God who is shaping our lives, as long as we remain in relationship with Him. And "his work is perfect." Deuteronomy 32:4.

Thesis 89

Perfection can be a dangerous topic if it focuses our attention on ourselves and our own works.

CAUTION: Studying the subject of perfection can be dangerous to your spiritual health!

We shouldn't avoid the study of perfection, however, for perfection *is* a Bible teaching. But it can be a dangerous study if it focuses our attention upon ourselves. Any time our attention is on ourselves, instead of upon Christ, we will fall and fail and sin. We can safely study perfection only when we remember that it is God's work in us, not our own work. And if perfection is God's work alone, then a study of perfection will focus our attention upon Him and away from ourselves.

The Bible describes three kinds of perfection. We can be perfect in birth, perfect in growth, and perfect in character. Sometimes you hear people discuss a text like Matthew 5:48, "Be ye therefore perfect, even as your Father which is in heaven is perfect." And they will say, "It doesn't mean 'perfect,' it means 'mature.' "

But *mature is* a stronger word than *perfect*. A baby can be a perfect baby as it gurgles and coos. A child can be a perfect child as he sits on the curb and goes "Blither, blither" to the neighbor children across the street. But if he were still behaving that way at age 20, we'd be concerned!

To be perfect in character is not only to be perfect in birth and in growth, but in maturity as well.

Mark 4:28 says, "First the blade, then the ear, after that the full corn in the ear." A blade can be a perfect blade; an ear can be a perfect ear. But the full corn in the ear means to be both

283

perfect and mature. *Christ's Object Lessons*, page 65, says that we can be perfect at every stage of our development.

So the Bible teaches that perfection is possible. The Bible also teaches that perfection is God's work, not ours, as we noticed in the previous chapter. And the Bible teaches that we should never claim to have perfection—in fact, such a claim would prove that we are *not* perfect! Job 9:20: "If I justify myself, mine own mouth shall condemn me: If I say, I am perfect, it shall also prove me perverse."

"No one who claims holiness is really holy. Those who are registered as holy in the books of heaven are not aware of the fact, and are the last ones to boast of their own goodness."—*The Faith I Live By*, p. 140. "The truly righteous man . . . is unconscious of his goodness and piety."—*The Sanctified Life*, p. 11. "The closer you come to Jesus, the more faulty you will appear in your own eyes; for your vision will be clearer, and your imperfections will be seen in broad and distinct contrast to His perfect nature. This is evidence that Satan's delusions have lost their power; that the vivifying influence of the Spirit of God is arousing you."—*Steps to Christ*, pp. 64, 65.

If the closer we get to Jesus, the less perfect we seem to be in our own estimation, then perfection can never be intended to capture our attention, for we won't know when we have received it. Our part in the process of perfection is to continue to draw close to Jesus and keep our eyes upon Him. He will take care of the rest.

"Each one will have a close struggle to overcome sin in his own heart. This is at times a very painful and discouraging work; because, as we see the deformities in our character, we keep looking at them, when we should look to Jesus and put on the robe of His righteousness."—*Testimonies*, vol. 9, pp. 182, 183.

But as long as we remember that perfection is God's work for us, and as long as we look to Him to accomplish whatever needs to be done in this area, we can safely study His promises about it. We can rejoice in the abundant provision He has made to reclaim us from sin.

Thesis 90

Jesus was like Adam before the fall in that He had a sinless nature—He was not born separated from God. Jesus was like Adam after the fall in physical strength, mental power, and moral worth (backbone).

People sometimes ask if Jesus was like Adam before the fall or like Adam after the fall. The answer is Yes!

In order to understand the answer, we have to understand what aspects of Jesus' life we are talking about. We might divide His personality as a human being into four aspects: spiritual nature, physical strength, mental power, and moral worth or backbone.

Jesus was like Adam before the fall in His spiritual nature. "Christ is called the second Adam. In purity and holiness, connected with God and beloved by God, *He began where the first Adam began.* Willingly *He passed over the ground where Adam fell*, and redeemed Adam's failure."—*S.D.A. Bible Commentary*, vol. 7A, p. 650.

Christ was completely human, but completely sinless—the only human being since Adam to be able to make such a claim. He could say, unchallenged, at the close of His ministry, "The prince of this world cometh, and hath nothing in me." John 14:30. *Selected Messages*, book 1, page 256 says: "We should have no misgivings in regard to the perfect sinlessness of the human nature of Christ." And Ellen G. White Comments, *S.D.A. Bible Commentary*, volume 7, page 912 says: "He was to take His position at the head of humanity by taking the nature but not the sinfulness of man."

At first glance, you may see a contradiction here, for there is a sense in which Christ took upon Himself our guilt, our sin, and even our sinful nature. Although He took our guilt, He did not become guilty, or He, too, would have needed a Saviour. When He took our sinful nature, it did not make His nature sinful. He took our guilt and sin as our Substitute.

When the angel came to visit Mary with the tidings of the Messiah soon to be born, he said, "The Holy Ghost shall come upon thee, and the power of the Highest shall overshadow thee: therefore also that holy thing which shall be born of thee shall be called the Son of God." Luke 1:35. Jesus was born differently from the way we are born. None of us could ever be called "that holy thing." Like Adam before the fall, Jesus had man's human nature, with the *possibility* of yielding to temptation. But since He never yielded to sin, He remained sinless. See *The Desire of Ages*, p. 117. Thus He became the second Adam and redeemed us from the failure of the first Adam. See 1 Corinthians 15: 21, 22.

But Jesus was also born differently from Adam. In the first place, he was born! Adam was not; Adam was created! But Jesus did not begin with the advantages with which Adam began. "For four thousand years the race had been decreasing in physical strength, in mental power, and in moral worth; and Christ took upon Him the infirmities of degenerate humanity. Only thus could He rescue man from the lowest depths of his degradation."—*The Desire of Ages*, p. 117.

So Christ accepted less physical strength than Adam had possessed. He was not as tall as Adam, for the race had been decreasing in size since the time of Creation. He was not as strong as Adam. He got tired and needed rest when Adam probably would not—such as that night on the lake and by the well in Samaria, times when even His disciples were able to keep going.

Christ the human was not as smart as Adam! The wisdom seen in His ministry came from above Him, not from within Him. He did not use His divine "IQ." He depended upon His Father for wisdom and even for His plans for each day.

Neither did Christ have the measure of moral worth that Adam had. What is moral worth? Ellen White, who used the term, did not define it. But moral worth has to do with how much backbone a person has, how much control over his behavior. If Christ had less moral worth than Adam, then He would have been weaker than Adam, less able to resist temptation in His human nature apart from power from above.

What a statement of the love of God, that He was willing to allow His Son to come and take such a risk in our behalf! *The Desire of Ages* tells us that the Father permitted Christ "to meet life's peril in common with every human soul, to fight the battle as every child of humanity must fight it, at the risk of failure and eternal loss." We long to shield our loved ones from Satan's power. But "to meet a bitterer conflict and a more fearful risk, God gave His only begotten Son, that the path of life might be made sure for our little ones. 'Herein is love.' Wonder, O heavens! and be astonished, O earth!"—Page 49.

Thesis 91

Jesus had no advantage over us in overcoming temptation.

In today's economy, many people find themselves having financial problems. If you find yourself among this group, you may wish to take a seminar entitled "How to Live Within Your Income." It's being taught by John D. Rockefeller. Are you interested? For students, how about a class called "Homework Made Easy." The teacher has an IQ of 200. Or do you prefer something in the field of sports? How about a class in Sky Diving—taught by the angel Gabriel?

If Jesus came to be our Saviour only, then it might not be so important how He lived His life. But if He came to be our example, to show us how to live, then He must live life as we have to live it. Otherwise, we wouldn't be able to profit by His example.

The Desire of Ages, page 24, says: "If we had to bear anything which Jesus did not endure, then upon this point Satan would represent the power of God as insufficient for us."

In all of the discussion and debate concerning the nature of Christ, two major points bring most of the disagreement: the question of what it means that Jesus was tempted in all points like we are, yet without sin (see Hebrews 4) and how Jesus could be born sinless of human parentage. Neither of these questions has direct application to our lives, and both are questions which we have been told are mysteries that we shouldn't spend a lot of time trying to figure out. See Ellen G. White Comments, *S.D.A. Bible Commentary*, vol. 5, pp. 1128, 1129.

On the other hand, almost everyone seems to agree on two other major points in this subject: that Jesus had no advantage over us in overcoming temptation and that He overcame sin in the same way in which we can overcome. These are practical points on which we have much inspired information.

Not even by a thought did Jesus yield to temptation—and the same victory may be ours as well. See *The Desire of Ages*, p. 123. Revelation 3:21 says that we can overcome in the same way in which Jesus overcame. "Through the victory of Christ the same advantages that he had are provided for man; for he may be a partaker of a power out of and above himself, even a partaker of the divine nature, by which he may overcome the corruption that is in the world through lust."—Ellen G. White, *Signs of the Times*, January 16, 1896.

So Jesus had no advantage over us in overcoming sin; therefore He is qualified to show us how to live. He came and experienced the needs and weaknesses of humanity so He could offer assistance to those who must live within the limits of humanity.

No doubt Jesus *possessed* all kinds of advantages over us, for He was God as surely as He was man. But He never *used* the advantages with which He was born, and as long as He did not use them, those very advantages gave Him an equal or greater *disadvantage* compared to us.

For instance, Jesus had a real advantage when it came to behavior, because having never sinned, He could never be tempted to *continue* in sin—and the momentum of transgression is one of our greatest downward pulls. On the other hand, He had a *disadvantage* when it came to relationship with His Father, for He had the inherent power to live life apart from dependence upon His Father—and we don't. Who has the greater temptation to live independently? The one who has the power to do so, or the one who does not?

The Ellen G. White Comments, *S.D.A. Bible Commentary*, volume 7, page 930, says: "It was a difficult task for the Prince of life to carry out the plan which He had undertaken for the salvation of man, in clothing His divinity with humanity. He had received honor in the heavenly courts, and was familiar with absolute power. It was as difficult for Him to keep the level of humanity as for men to rise above the low level of their depraved natures, and be partakers of the divide nature."

So when it came to the basic issue in sin and temptation—separation from a relationship with God—not only did Christ have no advantage over us, He actually had a disadvantage. "Man is not able to save himself, but the Son of God fights his battles for him, and places him on vantage-ground by giving him his divine attributes."—Ellen G. White, *Review and Herald*, February 8, 1898.

The life of Jesus is our assurance that we can overcome temptation. As He gained the victory through dependence upon His Father, so we may gain the victory through dependence upon Him. We can be on "vantage-ground" today.

Thesis 92

Jesus overcame temptation the same way we can overcome: by power from above rather than power from within.

Jesus had worked hard all day, teaching and healing the people. When evening came, He went with His disciples across the lake. He was exhausted. Hardly had they begun their journey when He fell asleep in the back of the boat.

The disciples hardly noticed. They were fishermen—not teachers. All day long Jesus had done His work; now it was time for them to do theirs. They might be awkward trying to minister to the people as He did, although they were learning. But things to do with the sea and ships were in their department, and they were confident they could handle whatever might happen.

They didn't worry about the storm at first. They had seen many storms on this particular sea, and they had weathered them all. Fighting to keep control of the boat absorbed their attention, and by the time the storm was at its worst, they had actually forgotten that Jesus was on board. It seems incredible, doesn't it? We wonder how they could have forgotten.

But how many times have we forgotten Jesus? Have you ever had it happen? Have you ever had a near-accident on the freeway and found yourself depending upon your driving skill to save you, rather than crying out for help from above? Have you ever been in a family crisis, when tempers were high and words were sharp, and you tried to calm the storm—and remembered to pray *afterward*? When one of your children is the victim of injury or sudden illness, whom do you call first—the family doctor or the Great Physician? It's possible even today for us to forget that Jesus is on board, isn't it?

The experience of Jesus and His disciples that night on the lake is a parable for us today of how Jesus overcame temptation. *The Desire of Ages*, page 336, describes it this way: "When Jesus was awakened to meet the storm, He was in perfect peace. There was no trace of fear in word or look, for no fear was in His heart. But He rested not in the possession of almighty power. It was not as the 'Master of earth and sea and sky' that He reposed in quiet. That power He had laid down, and He says, 'I can of Mine own self do nothing.' John 5:30. He trusted in the Father's might. It was in faith—faith in God's love and care— that Jesus rested, and the power of that word which stilled the storm was the power of God. As Jesus rested by faith in the Father's care, so we are to rest in the care of our Saviour."

Ellen White goes on to make the connection between the storm at sea and the storms of temptation that come upon us. "How often the disciples' experience is ours! When the tempests of temptation gather, and the fierce lightnings flash, and the waves sweep over us, we battle with the storm alone, forgetting that there is One who can help us. We trust to our own strength till our hope is lost, and we are ready to perish. Then we remember Jesus, and if we call upon Him to save us, we shall not cry in vain. Though He sorrowfully reproves our unbelief and self-confidence, He never fails to give us the help we need."— *Ibid.*

It is good news that Jesus overcame in the same way that we can overcome. It is good news because He lived life as we have to live it. He did not have an advantage over us in living His life of dependence upon His Father. It is good news because He gained the victory—and through Him we also can gain the victory. Through His justifying grace, His victory is placed to our account when we come to Him for forgiveness. But He makes more than vicarious victory available. Through His power in our lives, we can know His victory by experience as well. "Jesus revealed no qualities, and exercised no powers, that men may not have through faith in Him. His perfect humanity is that which all His followers may possess, if they will be in subjection to God as He was."—*Ibid.*, p. 664. And in *Selected Messages*, book 1, we find these words, "He [Christ] withstood the temptation, through the power that man may command. He laid hold on the throne of God, and there is not a man or woman who may not have access to the same help through faith in God. Man may become a partaker of the divine nature; not a soul lives who may not summon the aid of Heaven in temptation and trial. Christ came to reveal the source of His power, that man might never rely on his unaided human capabilities."—Page 409.

Christ laid down His divine power when He came to this earth. Yet it was through divine power that He was victorious. He gave up using His inherent divinity and depended instead upon power from above Him. And the same power is available to us. Divinity can be combined with humanity in our lives as it was in His, and by becoming "partakers of the divine nature," we can be overcomers. 2 Peter 1:4.

Thesis 93

Jesus found sins repulsive. So long as we depend on God, we also find sins repulsive.

Because Jesus lived His entire earthly life in dependence upon His Father, because He never gave in to the temptation to separate Himself from His Father, even for a moment, the devil was not able to tempt Him with sins, plural. He found sins repulsive.

The evidence is given, over and over again, in the inspired writings. Hebrews 1:9 says of Christ, "Thou hast loved righteousness, and hated iniquity." *The Desire of Ages*, page 111: "Every sin, every discord, every defiling lust that transgression had brought, was torture to His spirit." *Selected Messages*, book 1, page 322: "Hating sin with a perfect hatred, He [Jesus] yet gathered to His soul the sins of the whole world." Ellen G. White Comments—*S.D.A. Bible Commentary*, volume 5, page 1142: "His character revealed a perfect hatred for sin." Volume 7, page 904: "Christ ever retained the utmost hatred for sin." Volume 7, page 927: "Would that we could comprehend the significance of the words, Christ 'suffered being tempted.' While He was free from the taint of sin, the refined sensibilities of His holy nature rendered contact with evil unspeakably painful to Him." *The Desire of Ages*, page 88: Jesus "hated but one thing in the world, and that was sin. He could not witness a wrong act without pain which it was impossible to disguise." *The Desire of Ages*, page 700: Jesus "suffered in proportion to the perfection of His holiness and His hatred of sin. . . . To be surrounded by human beings under the control of Satan was revolting to Him."

Sometimes people will try to prove that Christ was tempted with evil in the same way in which a sinful man is tempted when he is living apart from Christ. They say that the sins and temptations that the devil brought to Christ in this world were attractive to Him, but that He gritted His teeth, stiffened His spine, and refused to act out that which His natural desires urged Him to do. Nothing could be further from the truth.

Another theory is that Christ was attracted by evil things, that He experienced lust and greed and anger, but that because of His love for His Father, He refused to do that which He would otherwise have been happy to do. The inspired information does not support this view either. While it is true that His love for His Father was strong, His hatred for sin was also strong. He found sin repulsive, not attractive.

As we study the life and nature of Christ, the good news is that His view of sin and wrong is also available for us. We don't have to live out our Christian lives wishing we could join the world in its sins, but gritting our teeth and forcing ourselves not to do so. We don't have to try to work up enough love for God so that we are willing to deny our natural instincts in order to make Him happy. We can experience the same kind of victory that Jesus experienced—victory not only over the sinful actions, but over the sinful desires as well. A victory that goes beyond behavior, to the very desires and tastes of the heart. We can find sins as repulsive as Jesus did.

Again, the evidence in the inspired writings is overwhelming. *Messages to Young People*, page 338: "When we are clothed with the righteousness of Christ, we shall have no relish for sin. . . . We may make mistakes, but we will hate the sin that caused the suffering of the Son of God." *The Great Controversy*, pages 649, 650: "By their own painful experience they learned the evil of sin, its power, its guilt, its woe; and they look upon it with abhorrence." *The Great Controversy*, page 508: "In the renewed heart there is hatred of sin." *Testimonies*, volume 2, page 294, speaks of the converted person: "His former life appears disgusting and hateful. He hates sin." And *The Desire of Ages*, page 668: "When we know God as it is our privilege to know Him, our life will be a life of continual obedience.

Through an appreciation of the character of Christ, through communion with God, sin will become hateful to us."

Do you relish sins, or do you find them disgusting and hateful? The difference comes in whether or not you know God as it is your privilege to know Him. You don't hate sin by trying hard to hate sin. You learn to hate sin by putting forth the necessary effort to know God and commune with Him day by day. No matter where you start in the study of salvation by faith in Jesus Christ, you always end up in the same place. Do you know Him? Knowing Him is the basis of all the things that follow. Knowing Him is life eternal.

Thesis 94

We can never *be* as Jesus was, but we can *do* as Jesus did.

Remember singing the song "I would Be Like Jesus"?

Be like Jesus, this my song,
In the home and in the throng;
Be like Jesus all day long!
I would be like Jesus.

Is it possible to be like Jesus? Or was that song a mistake? Is it possible to be like Jesus in some way and not in others?

To begin with, we know that there is one way in which we can never be like Jesus—for He is God and we are not. He is our Creator, and we are only creatures. We can become partakers of His divine nature through His indwelling presence in our lives. But we will never be more than human beings. So in that sense we can never be like Jesus.

"The incarnation of Christ has ever been, and will ever remain a mystery. That which is revealed, is for us and for our children, but let every human being be warned from the ground of making Christ altogether human, such an one as ourselves; for it cannot be."—Ellen G. White Comments, *S.D.A. Bible Commentary*, vol. 5, p. 1129.

But even when we limit our comparison to the human aspect of Jesus' nature, we still find that we can never be exactly like Him. He was born "that holy thing," *sinless* by nature from birth, as we noticed in Thesis 90. We were born separated from God, *sinful* by nature from birth. So long as we live in this world, we will have that difference in our very natures. See *Christ's Object Lessons*, page 160.

Another way in which we can never be like Jesus is in our sinful past. We have a bad track record. Throughout eternity we will always find ourselves in need of the justifying and pardoning grace of Christ to cover our past sins. Since Jesus never sinned, He never had a sinful past.

However, it is still possible for us to be like Jesus! We can live as Jesus lived and work as He worked. We can have the victory over temptations in the same way He did, through dependence upon a power from above, rather than a power from within. We can live in relationship to God as He lived and thus find that the differences between us make no difference!

Jesus lived as man. Throughout His entire life on this earth, He never used His divine power until the morning of the Resurrection.

All of the miracles that Jesus performed—raising the dead, healing the sick, cleansing the lepers, casting out demons, walking on water, reading people's minds—all were performed by His followers. The works that Jesus did were works done by His Father. Jesus said so in John 14:10, "The Father that dwelleth in me, he doeth the works."

About eleven times the book *The Desire of Ages* mentions that "divinity flashed through humanity." The first time was at the first cleansing of the temple, when for a moment the veil of humanity seemed to have slipped aside, and mankind saw a glimpse of the divinity within. But even there, the wording is significant. It says divinity flashed *through*—not *forth*. Even then, the Father was in control, and it was the Father's divinity that was revealed through His Son.

But even more important than the miracles that Jesus performed is the victory that He was given in His battle with the enemy. Through communion with His Father, through dependence upon His Father, He gained the victory. And His victory can be ours. Just as the Father's works were manifest in Jesus' life, so He can work in us, "to will and to do of his good pleasure." Philippians 2:13.

Thesis 95

The problem of sin is a broken relationship between God and man. The goal of salvation is to restore the relationship between God and man.

Jesus wants to get married! Revelation 19:6-9 tells us about it. "I heard as it were the voice of a great multitude, and as the voice of many waters, and as the voice of mighty thunderings, saying, Alleluia: for the Lord God omnipotent reigneth. Let us be glad and rejoice, and give honour to him: for the marriage of the Lamb is come, and his wife hath made herself ready. And to her was granted that she should be arrayed in fine linen, clean and white: for the fine linen is the righteousness of saints. And he saith unto me, Write, Blessed are they which are called unto the marriage supper of the lamb."

The relationship between mankind and God was broken in Eden. When Adam and Eve sinned, they hid themselves and no longer came eagerly to meet God; no longer could they walk with Him in the cool of the evening.

Adam and Eve had chosen not to trust the One who had been only trustworthy, and thus the relationship with God was broken.

But God was not willing that the story should end there. Communion with His created children was so important to Him that He was willing to go to the cross in order to restore that broken relationship. He came personally to walk among men, this time veiled with humanity, in order to bridge the gap that sin had made.

"Since Jesus came to dwell with us, we know that God is acquainted with our trials, and sympathizes with our griefs. Every son and daughter of Adam may understand that our Creator is the friend of sinners. For in every doctrine of grace, every promise of joy, every deed of love, every divine attraction presented in the Saviour's life on earth, we see 'God with us.' "—*The Desire of Ages*, p. 24.

And now Jesus wants to get married. What does it mean to get married? It means to get together personally and permanently.

In the Tokyo airport my wife and I once met a Swedish man on his way to meet his bride in Seoul, Korea. They had never met. They had done a lot of long-distance communication through correspondence. But this was the first time they would see each other in person. He was understandably eager to meet her. He was looking forward to the marriage, looking forward to getting together with her in person and for keeps.

Through prayer and the study of His Word, we have been in correspondence with Jesus. We have learned to love Him, because He first loved us. But we can join Him in looking forward to the marriage, to the time when we can meet with Him, personally and forever.

Sometimes people worry about a day-by-day relationship with Christ becoming just another works trip. But the relationship is not simply a means to an end. It is the end itself! We do not have a relationship with Christ in order to be saved. We are saved in order to be able to have a relationship with Christ!

"As through Jesus we enter into rest, heaven begins here. We respond to His invitation, Come, learn of Me, and in thus coming we begin the life eternal. Heaven is a ceaseless approaching to God through Christ. The longer we are in the heaven of bliss, the more and still more of glory will be opened to us; and the more we know of God, the more intense will be our happiness. As we walk with Jesus in this life, we may be filled with His love, satisfied with His presence. All that human nature can bear, we may receive here. But what is this compared with the hereafter?"—*The Desire of Ages*, pp. 331, 332.

Jesus wants to get married! Do you?